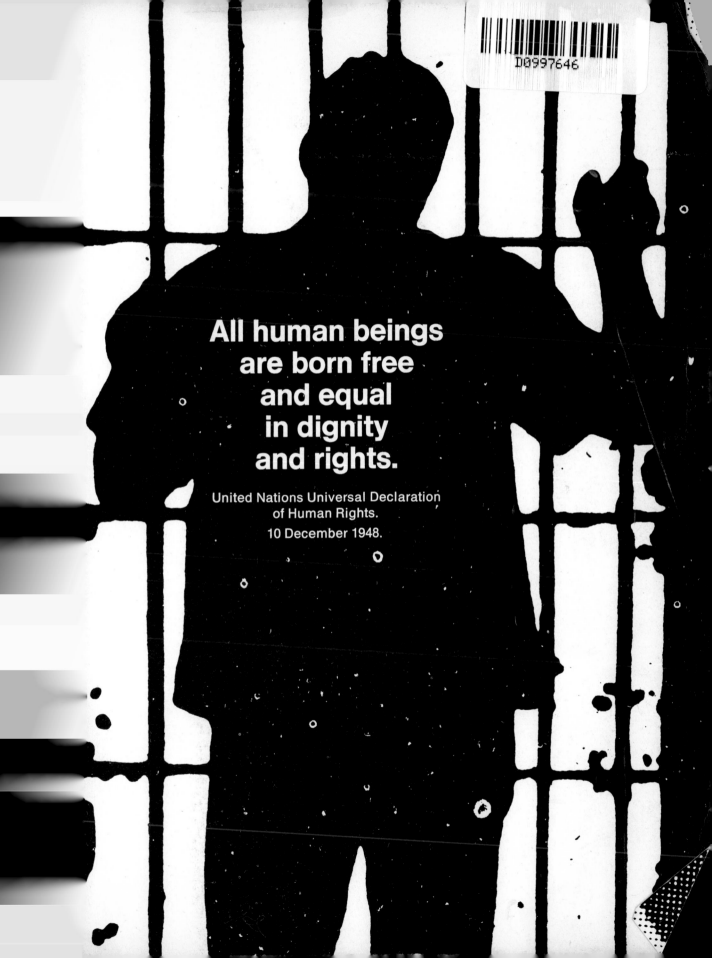

All human beings
are born free
and equal
in dignity
and rights.

United Nations Universal Declaration
of Human Rights.
10 December 1948.

Peter Chippindale and Ed Harriman

JUNTAS UNITED!

QUARTET BOOKS

LONDON   MELBOURNE   NEW YORK

First published by
Quartet Books Limited 1978
A member of the Namara Group
27 Goodge Street, London W1P 1FD

Copyright © 1978 by
Peter Chippindale and Ed Harriman

ISBN 0 7043 3211 6

Design by Mike Jarvis
Cover illustration by Lez Gibbard
Typeset by Bedford Typesetters Limited

Printed in England by Hunt Barnard Web Offset Ltd.

FOREWORD

This book cuts a swathe across the political system – from Fascist to Marxist-Leninist. It is about hundreds of millions of people who today live under tyrannical régimes.

The varying harshness of the régimes does not matter to many of them. They are too busy just staying alive. To others, who have risen above subsistence level and can expect to live beyond the age of forty, have an income, and read and write, who rules on their behalf is a matter of passionate debate and demonstration.

Anybody who picks this book up should bear in mind that they live in a relatively free country. Few military régimes allow their subjects to read anything which is critical or not their version of the truth.

The authors do not pretend this is a definitive work on the subject of military dictatorships. But they hope it will lead to a greater understanding of the type of world we all live in, and of hard realities which should not be ignored. However ludicrous or impossibly cruel the leaderships and the events may seem, they have been, and are, happening.

We would have liked to include many more countries. Ecuador – where the last counter-coup was stalled by a traffic jam; Burma – where the military quickly changed into civilian clothes; Libya – where petty thieves have their hands chopped off; Namibia – where South Africa uses torture and troops to stay in control.

Time, space and other constrictions have prevented us. Add your own as you wish.

We would like to thank all the people who have helped us.

Peter Chippindale
Ed Harriman
London, 1978

ARGENTINA

General Jorge Videla, Commander-in-Chief of the Army and President of Argentina, is said to wear black gloves in public because he bites his nails. From this, it might be concluded that there is hope for democracy in Argentina yet. His gloves can be seen every time he salutes – which he does frequently, to military parades, visiting heads of state, football crowds, and on occasion even to lamp-posts. He is not a puppet. Just a very austere, threadbare man. He has a frumpish wife. And at his own inauguration, he cut the ceremony short, wore an ordinary uniform and prohibited applause. The Argentinian press was full of stories about his frugal past, a family man living on a modest military stipend. The Americans say he is 'moderate', in comparison with Admiral Massera, another junta member, whose high living and anti-communism even by Buenos Aires standards are bizarre and extreme. Videla has not been among the generals who condone bombing synagogues, publicly calling for a 'final solution' to Argentina's half million Jews. But he has been doing well enough that as host to the World Cup his exploits deserve to be known.

In the three years since he took over in a coup on 24 March 1975, more than 15,000 men and women have disappeared from the streets in Argentina. Some 10,000 are in gaol, not as 'political prisoners', but as 'subversive criminals' according to the official terminology.

Four thousand people have been killed. Lawyers have filed over 20,000 writs of habeas-corpus, asking the government where people who disappeared are. But they have had few answers. Videla, moderate though he may be, presides over one of the most bloody dictatorships in the world. Corpses turn up along roadsides at dawn, mutilated beyond recognition.

General Videla, the 'moderate'
Keystone Press

Gustavo Ponce de Leon with his wife and family in their Buenos Aires flat.
One of thousands who disappeared after being taken away by the police

Others are found blown to pieces in quarries, floating in rivers, lakes, decomposing on rubbish tips, marked with cigarette burns, rope abrasions, their toe-nails missing, eyes gouged out and hands cut off to avoid identification. Buenos Aires residents only hear the occasional rattle of machine-gun fire. But Videla is well aware of what is going on. 'This is really war,' he said. 'In a war there are survivors, wounded, dead and sometimes people who disappear.' Actually, for him it is more of a crusade.

'It is a serious crime to assault our Western and Christian style of life and try to change it into something we do not like,' he declared. 'If the army has to take the responsibility of guiding the country, we are going to end the venality, the chaos and disorder once and for all.'

Amnesty International has dossiers of affidavits from people who have been abducted off the streets, taken to barracks, and yet somehow survived Videla's war. They describe people having their heads held under water till near drowning (*el submarino*), electric shocks applied with the *picana* (prod) to the most sensitive parts of their bodies, toe-nails pulled out. Rats have been put on fresh wounds. Women are raped, sometimes by police dogs. They have seen fellow inmates savaged by the dogs, frozen to death at night and, as is common throughout much of Latin America, 'shot while trying to escape'. Many of the murders and torture were attributed to the AAA – Anti-Communist Alliance, a secret death squad which operate with a remarkably free hand, in close collaboration with the military. Many death squad members today are active soldiers.

Videla described the death squads as 'an undesirable reality'. His foreign minister, Admiral Cesar Guzzetti, went further. After speaking at the United Nations he said: 'My idea of subversion

Buenos Aires – the bosses

is that of left-wing terrorist organizations. Subversion or terrorism of the right is not the same thing. When the social body of the country has been contaminated by a disease that corrodes its entrails, it forms antibodies. These antibodies cannot be considered in the same way as microbes. As the government controls and destroys the guerilla, the action of the antibody will disappear, as is already happening.'

One of Videla's other generals, commander of the Third Army Corps based in Córdoba, Argentina's second largest city where several World Cup matches are played, is more blunt. Motto: 'While Videla rules, I kill.'

The Argentine parliament has been closed since the coup, opposition senators and deputies figure prominently among those imprisoned, killed and forced into exile. Trade unions are run by the military, and the press is censored. Over 100,000 professional people – lecturers, scientists, technicians – have fled overseas. Buenos Aires' once fine bookshops are now filled with trash. Isabel Perón, the feeble woman Videla deposed, lies in a Naval prison, hoarding barbiturates for periodic suicide attempts.

But Videla is building a 'stable, strong modern democracy,' states the official government magazine which is full of glossy photographs of steaks, tangos, and beautiful women on beaches. 'The Foreign Investment Law, decreed in February 1977, guarantees full remittance of profits and capital without limit,' it reads.

The Finance Minister, José Alfredo Martinez de Hoz, is a close childhood friend of David Rockefeller, Chairman of Chase Manhattan Bank. Martinez de Hoz is also one of Argentina's largest landowners, director of a steel firm, two large insurance companies, two construction firms, Pan-American Airways, Western Telegraph Company, the utility Italo-Argentina de Electrici-

Night-life in Buenos Aires

dad, president of a finance house and adviser to Exxon and Siemens. He has reduced wages to a level that the Minister of Labour has publicly said is too low to live on, and called for half a million government employees to be sacked by 1981. In some areas of Buenos Aires one out of three infants die in the first year. Some people are fighting back – with strikes, industrial sabotage, and silent vigils by women whose husbands and sons have disappeared.

Videla has some strange friends. Last year he helped the Argentine Communist Party arrange an anniversary dinner in a downtown Buenos Aires hotel. In return, Luis Corvalan, head of the banned Chilean Communist Party and now in Moscow, refuses publicly to condemn Videla's régime. Even Fidel Castro carefully leaves Argentina off his list of repressive Latin American states.

But the twenty-five million Argentinians have no choice but to condition themselves for the second stage of the junta's programme – a programme for 'modifying political habits and methods of selecting political leaders', government press releases explain. The new enemies, Videla says, are 'the authors of political subversion . . . who do not use bombs, but who create far more damage because they destroy the mind'. First the crusade. Now the inquisition. And as Videla is ostensibly the military's intellectual, it is not surprising that he should be leading it as well.

Generals Menendez and Bussi discussing how to defend 'Christianity and the Western Way of Life', in the Argentinian countryside *Gamma*

BANGLADESH

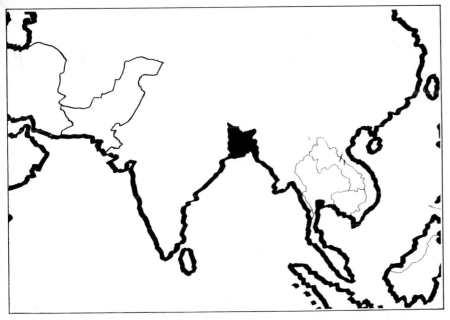

Major-General Ziaur Rahman rules Bangladesh with a combination of martial law and massive subsidies from Western governments in the form of foreign aid.

He is also the only leader to have sanctioned the political death sentence in Dacca, the capital, for forty years. The first man who hanged, after a secret, in camera, Special Martial Law Tribunal, on 21 July 1976, was Colonel Abu Taher, the man who nine months earlier had saved Ziaur's life by rescuing him from other plotting officers in a flurry of coups and counter-coups.

Five years earlier the two together rallied the Bangladeshi armies and people to fight off Pakistani armies which began a pogrom of wanton slaughter,

One third of food aid to Bangladesh goes to feed the middle classes. The urban poor must pay inflated prices, steal, or starve

rape and looting in the country on 25 March 1971.

The Bangladeshi (or Bengali) people had voted themselves into existence as a nation by giving the Awami League party, led by Sheikh Mujibur Rahman, enough seats to have an absolute majority in the national assembly of what was then combined East and West Pakistan. The Awami League campaigned on a programme of national autonomy for the East (Bangladesh), drawing on popular resentment from the blatant profiteering and corruption of officials (most from the West) involved in distributing aid following the 1970 cyclone in which at least 200,000 Bengalis died. But General Yahya Khan, President of Pakistan, could never allow the country to be split. So when orders to massacre the Bengalis reached the barracks where Taher was stationed in the West, he immediately fled across to India to raise guerilla armies among his people in the East.

On 26 March, Ziaur went on the radio and declared Bangladesh independent.

Bangladesh is the part of Asia the rest of the world ignored for decades. When Clive of India entered Dacca after defeating the Bengalis in 1757, he was amazed. 'This city', he said, 'is as extensive, populous and rich as the City of London.' But since 1947, when it was cut off from India by partition, the country has been systematically exploited by government officials and bankrupted by businessmen, mostly from West Pakistan.

Dacca lapsed into a sprawling humid slum, where the main economic activity was smuggling. Though producing half the world's jute, and having one of the most sophisticated literatures in the world, the eighty million Bengalis there have been kept miserably poor. The most overcrowded country in the world, people earn on average seventy dollars a year, and one out of eight infants dies soon after birth, partly because there is only one doctor for

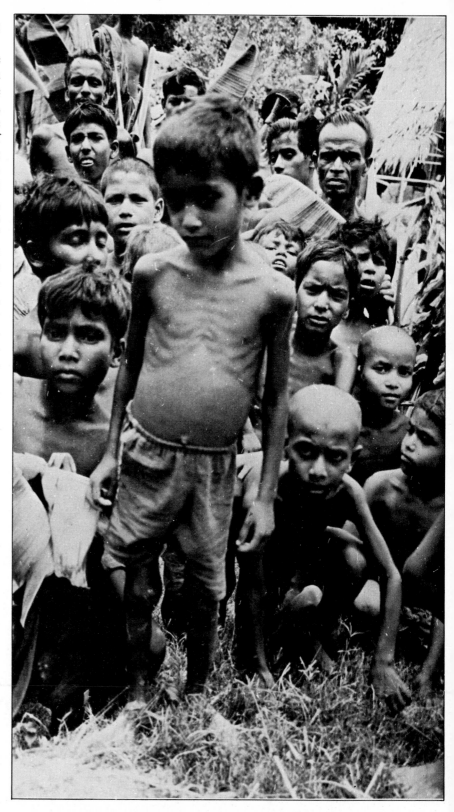

In the early 70s familes in refugee camps committed suicide rather than die slowly of starvation while relief ships refused to unload rice due to political pressures

18

President Ziaur Rahman had the man who saved his life condemned to death and hanged in Dacca Central Gaol

every ten thousand people, but mostly due to chronic malnutrition. In 1943 there was widespread starvation caused, according to the official report, by rice speculators and the tariff policies of the then British administration.

In 1971 after the Indian armies encircled the Pakistani force, obtained their surrender, and allowed Sheikh Mujibur to become head of the new state, they immediately stripped the country of virtually every movable piece of military and government equipment – tanks, typewriters, water coolers and light-bulbs.

Yet over the next three years more than 2.5 billion dollars of foreign aid was made available to Mujibur's government, most of it from the West, more than all Germany received under the Marshall Plan after the Second World War. Much of the credit and provisions was allocated under the name of humanitarian relief. Bangladesh was callously called 'the world's basket case'. Yet the donor countries were just as concerned to stabilize Mujibur's régime, and prevent the country from moving towards revolution or making a definite break with the West. Mujibur, though, astounded his supporters by the manner in which monies were channelled into his family's hands, and the

coffers of his Awami party. He also appointed his brother-in-law to control all appointments in the civil service, by far the country's largest employer.

Whereas in 1971 he could draw audiences of hundreds of thousands, three years later he kept mostly to his home. His response to growing popular discontent was to usurp arbitrary powers, declaring a State of Emergency in December 1974, allowing arrest without warrant and banning public meetings. He also closed newspapers except for those under government control, made himself President, outlawed all parties except the Awami League, and promulgated a law allowing unlimited detention of government opponents.

Then, following flooding after heavy monsoon rains, people began starving, not so much for lack of rice – though production fell by one-quarter, as from its high price pushed up by speculation and hoarding, devaluation of the currency, and the United States' refusal to extend an aid credit because Bangladesh was selling jute to Cuba.

Peasants rioted in land offices, pushing in queues to sell their land for meals. People in famine relief camps committed suicide rather than slowly starve. Rice cost five times as much as it had only a few years before. So in August 1975, Mujibur and his family were assassinated in a coup directed by six young majors with a regiment of Russian T-54 tanks, who immediately declared martial law and banned the Awami League.

That November Ziaur was under arrest by other officers who briefly assumed power after another putsch.

Abu Taher came to his rescue, and then set about mobilizing the militia in what became the first soldiers' rising since the Sepoy Mutiny in 1857. Ziaur was quickly installed by the soldiers and became Chief Martial Law Administrator. And two weeks later, Taher found himself duped into going peacefully to gaol. For his trial the following July, the Dacca Central Gaol was reinforced with sandbags, machine-guns and metal sheeting. He was hanged

Bangladesh used to export rice. Yet famines have been caused by hoarding, and graft by government officials following natural calamities

two days after verdict was passed, in secret. Since then Ziaur has remorselessly strengthened his grip, while at the same time introducing a credit system, capital market, and investment guidelines according to World Bank blueprints, making Bangladesh a test case for the Bank's Third World national development plans.

The country is now the fourth largest recipient of United States foreign aid, after Egypt, Indonesia and India. Ziaur has had the Constitution changed, returning Bangladesh from a secular to a Muslim state, and has toured the oil-rich Middle East.

Economically the country was and is being managed better than before.

Politically it has become unrecognizable from other dictatorships around the world.

The Special Powers Act of 1974 and the Martial Law of 1975 are still in force. Political parties are again legal, but only those which the government approves, and they are allowed only to meet indoors and issue press statements. Most of the opposition is squarely behind bars. The head of the Socialist Party is in solitary confinement. The reputable Bengali paper *Ittefaq* estimates there are as many as 53,000 political prisoners, either held on no charges at all or sentenced for criminal offences of 'a political nature'.

Ziaur is army Chief of Staff, Chief Martial Law Administrator, and made himself President in August last year, announcing that elections would be held, in which he may run. But neither he nor his security forces are confidently secure. On 22 June 1977, prison guards in Dacca Central Gaol rioted after the alarm bell went off, leaving over 3,000 of the 5,000 inmates badly beaten.

In October over 230 troops were killed when two attempted coups were put down. The newspapers were full of headlines such as: 'FOIL DESIGNS OF THE ENEMY', 'ANYONE STANDING IN THE WAY OF PROGRESS WILL BE CRUSHED', 'IDENTIFY STRANGERS', 'EXEMPLARY PUNISHMENT TO CONSPIRATORS'. Then came the executions of ordinary soldiers. The number sentenced to death by secret tribunals is unknown. People living near Dacca cantonment, the headquarters, reported frequently hearing volleys of rifle shots – firing squads – in the middle of the night. Men were hanged in Dacca Central Gaol.

Thirty per cent of food aid to Bangladesh goes to the urban middle classes. Thirty-five per cent goes to feeding the army. A sophisticated police communications system is now being installed. British counter-insurgency experts are setting up an officers' training school. The United States is training officers as well. The police force has been doubled. And the military and police spend thirty per cent of the government's budget.

In the country's south-east, Ziaur is waging war against tribal hill people. Over 12,000 troops are involved, and daily there are reports of looting, rape and killing. All this is paid for out of international aid, which donors have often insisted is nothing more than charitable relief.

Dacca. Probably the hottest, most humid capital in the world. At night volleys of rifle-fire – firing squads – are heard near the Central Gaol

BENIN

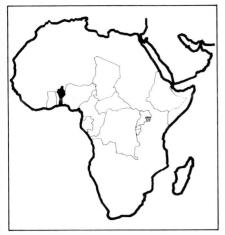

Benin used to hold the record for running through governors when it was the French colony of Dahomey. Twenty-six came and went in fifty years. The tradition continued after independence – nine presidents and three republics in a decade.

Lieutenant-Colonel Mathieu Kerecou is now changing that, still in power after his coup (the seventh) in October 1972, and having ushered in the 'scientific socialism' of Marxist-Leninist military rule, aided by the Benin People's Revolutionary Party.

Before he grabbed command all sorts of solutions were tried to solve the regionalism and tribalism which divide the three million population into three main groups. The Government of National Unity proclaimed at independence in 1960 lasted four months, the first President, Hubert Maga, long enough to build a £1 million palace known locally as 'Maga's folly'.

In 1968 a peculiar system of a rotating troika of civilian presidents was proposed to solve the differences between the Maga (north), Ahomad (south-west) and Apithy (south-east). It dissolved in chaos after the regional parties organized a successful boycott. The army instead installed a 'fourth man', Dr Emile-Herlin Zinsou, who hung on for a year before being deposed in a coup.

The three presidential candidates were recalled from Paris where they had been relaxing comfortably in exile and there was another try.

The security forces demanded that voting be staggered over three weeks, but their condition was not needed. As the campaign started so did violence and intimidation. The Military Triumvirate first suspended, then scrapped the whole proceedings and named a three-man Presidential Council with each of the candidates taking two-year terms of office as President. Maga started off first, but Kerecou then took over, calling for 'self-reliance to free the country from foreign domination' and bringing in new plans to replace earlier efforts like the first five-year plan which was so over-ambitious it had to be totally abandoned.

The small West African state has problems familiar to the area – almost hopeless economic prospects, a chronic imbalance between exports (eighty per cent palm products) and imports, a population of eighty-seven per cent peasantry and practically no industry.

Urging on his subjects, he has been looking to the Chinese to break away from almost total economic dependence on the French, who provided half the considerable aid for road-building, education and communications in 1974, and were buying seventy-five per cent of the exports. Today the country is a mass of Chinese construction sites and Chinese overseers organizing the peasants' labours in the fields.

Meanwhile he has been having his own problems at home. In 1976 the Revolutionary Council sentenced eleven people to death after finding them guilty of a plot to reinstate the deposed 'fourth man' (and previous army choice), Dr Zinsou.

The previous year he had a more

Don't shoot the natives. Modern white hunters

21

Tour of shacks

A.M. on the bumpy tarmac of Cotonou airport. Out jumped eighty mercenaries, two-thirds of them Europeans, who sauntered through the palm groves to a building 150 yards from the presidential palace, where they fired off mortars and machine-guns in a desultory fashion, taking the occasional break for a cigarette. After a couple of hours they packed up, paused for a drink in the grounds of the Hotel de la Croix du Sud, wandered back to their aircraft and flew off at eleven A.M., disappearing entirely.

Kerecou was on the radio within an hour of their arrival, announcing 'a vast plot of international imperialism' and urging 'militants' to defend Benin against 'this diabolical assault'.

A UN investigation established that seven people had died, including a civilian who, responding to his President's impassioned goadings, was cut down whilst wielding a machete from a bicycle. It pinned the blame on 'Force Omega', led by the Popular Front for the Liberation and Rehabilitation of Benin, whose leader had been sitting in the plane surrounded by heaps of three-page leaflets entitled 'Children of Dahomey, Arise! The Tyrant Is No More'.

Kerecou has now claimed twenty-eight million dollars' compensation from France, Gabon and Morocco (where it has been claimed the mercenaries were trained in the desert near Marrakesh). Morocco has hotly denied the allegations.

And at home he has been doing very well. A week later a ship arrived from China with thousands of T-shirts showing a picture of a mercenary holding a machine-gun and celebrating the 'glorious victory' of 16 January. They have been distributed to the locals, and Kerecou himself, so early on the state radio and highly satisfied with the minimum damage to his palace, is still cashing in on the kudos of his famous triumph in repulsing the fiendish invaders.

personal problem when he burst into the home of the Minister of the Interior to find him naked in the arms of his wife. The unfortunate Captain, who had obviously been taking his interior responsibilities too far, was promptly executed by the Presidential Guard. A government communiqué explained the shooting as 'because the nation's revolution demands good morals'. Questions by journalists about Mrs Kerecou, about whom little is known, were discouraged.

A more curious incident took place in January 1977 when a dilapidated propeller-driven aircraft landed at seven

The busy railway network

BOLIVIA

General Hugo Banzer Suárez, President of Bolivia since he seized power with arms air-lifted in from Brazil in 1971, has been sitting on top of the world. Literally. La Paz, the capital of the land-locked state which Brazilian financiers would like to see push through either Chile or Peru to a seaport of the Pacific coast, is 13,000 feet above sea level. Yolanda, Banzer's wife, is known among the populace for demanding the sacking of officials who get in her way. And with his brother-in-law the ambassador to Brazil, and his brother, Consul to La Plata, Argentina, Banzer keeps well informed about the lucrative narcotics trade between the three countries. Government receptions and dinner parties regularly feature in the heavily censored press. So when Banzer declared last July that he would vacate the presidency to move on to a loftier position as supreme guarantor of Bolivia's security and future, few Bolivians were surprised by the tone he assumed.

'Placing myself at the exact level of history and of my conscience,' he began, 'I do solemnly declare my decision to decline my candidacy for the Constitutional Presidency of the Nation . . . From now on my work and my strife get a new sense. I undertake the responsibility of devoting myself to the unity of the people, endeavouring to compatibilize the contradictions that arise out of them.'

Businessmen drinking coffee in cafés in the country's commercial centre, Santa Cruz, questioned whether this was a gesture of historical magnanimity, to cover up his failure to swap some mineral-rich Bolivian mountains for a corridor through Chile to the sea. Or did Banzer think he would lose as a candidate if he ran himself?

Eighty per cent of Bolivia's five million people are Indians. They speak their own languages instead of Spanish, and work in such servile conditions that Bolivia is called the Rhodesia of Latin America. Bolivia is also known as the country where ex-Nazis and German Jews get on best together. Characteristically, the white immigrant settler community, which accepts racism towards the Indians as a matter of course, has grown considerably richer in the past five years, particularly those families owning large estates on the country's eastern plain, of whom Banzer's in-laws are among the most well-heeled.

The landowners, called 'the Santa Cruz mob', support Banzer in return for generous government 'incentives' to chop down forests, plant cotton and sugar and graze cattle to sell overseas, all financed by cheap Brazilian loans.

The peons who do all the work are

'El Excelentisimo', General Hugo Banzer, as he likes to be seen

Waiting for Banzer to step down

rounded up in lorries by men who also sell them household goods and alcohol on credit when prices are highest – keeping them perpetually in debt, and often drunk. In northern Bolivia, Indians working on rubber plantations are locked up and handcuffed at night.

The region is virtually inaccessible except by canoe on closely guarded rivers, so company stores sell goods, like bars of soap, at over one hundred times their cost in La Paz. In 1976 over twenty Indians tried to escape, according to the Anti-Slavery Society. But they were captured after the owner called the police.

Banzer's nominee for the presidency, Air Force General Juan Pereda Asbun, was advised that it was important to be seen in villages on Bolivia's high central plateau, the altiplano, and the nearby

Cochambamba valleys, where the army has relied on peasant support since it divided the land among them in 1952. To help matters, the United States Agency for International Development (USAID) agreed to provide a 19.5 million dollar loan, which Banzer pledged would be spent and paid for by them.

But Pereda became unnerved when he addressed crowds of peasants. And he had trouble pronouncing the all-important, if slightly pretentious word, 'constitucionalizacion' – the whole legal basis upon which the election was called. The army do not like him, preferring their own generals to distribute contracts and promotions and bribes. And Santa Cruz landowners were noticeably ruffled that cash crop, cattle-raising and oil production all declined appreciably

last year.

But Banzer has been president longer than all but one of his predecessors in Bolivia's 150-year history.

He was trained by the United States Army, and was military attaché in Washington, before the coup – since when he has ruled by decree. The security forces have an almost free hand, and habeas-corpus is systematically denied. On 26 May 1976, his most serious rival, deposed president José Torres, was found dead by the roadside sixty miles outside Buenos Aires, Argentina. Two months later Banzer went to Argentina to see General Jorge Videla, head of the Argentine junta, on a friendship tour. It is not known whether they discussed Torres' death.

Yet recently the little dictator – he is

Two soldiers killed by guerillas. Che Guevara was caught and shot in Bolivia. Now forests are being cleared to make way for white settlers from Rhodesia

five feet, five inches tall – has been giving the impression of losing his touch, blundering over what started as a modest hunger strike by six families for the release of their men held as political prisoners last winter, which rapidly spread into a nation-wide vigil in churches by over 1,300 people. Banzer equivocated, tried to negotiate and then backed down. The police, fed up, smashed into the churches, dragging away the hunger strikers. Bolivia's bishops took offence. And no sooner were the political prisoners released than outlawed union leaders marched into their old union offices in broad daylight and bodily expelled Banzer's official nominees. All-important are the out-lawed miners' unions representing the 80,000 Indians who dig tin out of the highest and most expensive to run mines in the world. As the state mining company, COMIBOL, says in its twenty-fifth anniversary report: 'Mining, the principal base of the state's financial strategy, the irreplaceable plat-form for the welfare of a noble people such as are the Bolivians, formed with high spiritual values, rises once again, having overcome the disturbing stages caused by lack of conscience, vision and justice.' This refers to events in June two years ago, when COMIBOL agreed to see the outlawed leaders one day, and the government locked them up the day before. Over one thousand miners

Without copper from the Andes mountains shipped to England, Bolivia would be bankrupt

Men working in Bolivia's mines have a life expectancy of thirty years

A highway high in the Andes mountains

were gaoled. Troops occupied the mines which they have only recently left. And COMIBOL stores were closed, forcing the miners and their families to live on bread and tea.

Decree Law No. 11947, which prohibits strikes, is still in force. Banzer can send anyone who refuses work to prison or exile for two years. All the tin is refined by Rio Tinto Zinc in its factory outside Liverpool, England.

If the mines stop, the exchequer dries up. The Indian miners earn little more than a dollar a day, and are so blighted by silicosis that their average life expectancy is thirty years.

Banzer insists their strikes are caused by 'subversive elements'. His reasoning has been accepted by the Rhodesian government with whom he has been negotiating for 150,000 white Rhodesians to emigrate to Bolivia, setting aside 250 million dollars to help them. He wants them 'to share the perspective that

corresponds to our culture and our desires, that rests upon the genuine nature of the people'.

Whatever that may be 'el supremo' wants to determine himself. Last year a Bolivian newspaper published a list of generals due to retire. Banzer was on it. The newspaper's editor promptly received several death threats and his car was bombed. A successful war against Chile would recapture for Banzer much of his flagging sense of manifest destiny.

BRAZIL

'In October 1976, in the remote province of Mato Grosso, in the small township of Riberao Bonito, a priest, Father Joao Bosco Peindo Burnier, was shot by police when he went to protest about the torture of two women in the local police station. It is difficult to estimate how common such practices are since the victims, naturally, rarely file complaints. However, some idea of the extent can be got from an examination of the police figures for the number of people detained on suspicion alone in Sao Paulo in the first two months of 1977. There were 28,000 of them.'

Amnesty International

Brazil is the land of the Samba, Carnival and effervescent evenings in Rio. It is also the land of the *pau de arara* (parrot's perch), the dragon chair, and the pianola Boilenson – bizarre methods of torture.

Boilenson is thought to have founded OBAN, *Operacao Bandierantes*, in 1969 with army, navy and police officers. It is the São Paulo death squad. The keys of his pianola are linked to electric

Ernesto Geisel, President. Not known for his smile

wires which are attached to sensitive parts of a 'suspect's' body. When the pianola is played, an electric current is produced. The dragon chair is used for real and mock executions. The *pau de arara* involves hanging a person naked by their knees, and then beating them and giving electric shocks. The sworn affidavits which Amnesty International have about what goes on in Brazil's torture chambers are too unspeakably vivid to repeat. Amnesty has a list of over one thousand men and women who have endured it. It has published a list of eighty-six people who swore they were tortured under Sergio Fleury, who is both Commissioner (delgado) of the official São Paulo Department of Political and Social Order (DOPS) and chief of the death squad. Earlier this year, Fleury's reply to a letter written by a French church group asking him to stop was published.

'I know you, and those like you,' he wrote, 'who run away terrified and

The police go shopping in São Paulo

The Brazilian military celebrating its continuous rule since 1964 *Gamma*

wet their pants back stage . . . Don't excite yourself my little man . . . You are subverting the established order. I am defending it.'

So too are the Brazilian police trained and equipped by the United States Government, largely through the Public Assistance Programme of the United States Agency for International Development. In Rio de Janeiro, employees in the US Naval Mission have heard screams from the torture rooms of the police offices next door. Yet when asked by the United States Senate Committee, the past head of the United States Public Safety Mission in Brazil

An intimate view of the police, as seen by student demonstrators in Rio de Janeiro last year. The students were calling for liberalization of the régime
Gamma

claimed he knew nothing about the torture.

Brazil is the paradigm 'national security state'. 'Development and Security' is the motto. As Nixon said in 1971, 'Latin America will go where Brazil goes'. The government provided torturers for the Chilean junta in 1973, arms for Hugo Banzer's coup in Bolivia in 1971, and DOPS agents helped the Uruguayan military come to power.

President is General Ernesto Geisel. Trained at Fort Leavenworth, Kansas, he returned to Brazil in 1945 to lead troops who surrounded the residential palace in a coup replacing Getulio Vargas. Three days earlier the American ambassador publicly said Vargas should be overthrown.

In 1964 Geisel was a principal conspirator in the coup which overthrew President João Goulart. Then the United States sent congratulations to the generals even before Goulart was deposed.

In 1969 Geisel was appointed head of the state oil company, Petrobrás, where he sold the petro-chemical sector to foreign multi-nationals, and virtually stopped exploration in Brazil. General Vernon Walters, deputy director of the CIA, canvassed among Brazil's generals on Geisel's behalf, and in 1974 he was appointed president.

At his first cabinet meeting Geisel declared: 'The strengthening of national security is identical to that of national development itself . . . What the very dignity of the Federal Power cannot and

ust not allow is abusive and men-
acious criticism, or insistent and
nproper pressures coming from those
ithout any responsibilities for public
rvice.'

Even the Bolshoi Ballet has been
anned from Brazilian television. On
e other hand Rio is the safe asylum
r escaped international criminals,
cluding Ronald Biggs, the 'Great
rain' robber.

In April 1977, Geisel suspended the
razilian congress because the only
ficial opposition party, the Brazilian
emocratic Movement (MBD), refused
retract its insistence that habeas-
rpus for political 'suspects' be re-
ored. Without habeas-corpus police
e free to detain and torture at will, as
azilians well know. It and other civil
liberties are suspended under the 1968
Institutional Act No. 5.

Geisel also set out to ensure that his
National Revival Party (ARENA) is
guaranteed victory in the elections this
year. Simply by changing the electoral
rules – there are now not to be any
campaigns for state governorships, and
campaigning is allowed for only one-
third of the Brazilian Senate seats. No
candidate is allowed to discuss campaign
issues on radio or television, as Geisel
said in the past, 'to avoid confusing
the voters'.

When MBD leaders responded with
an unprecedented television attack,
Geisel unseated their leader from
the Chamber of Deputies and divested
him of all political rights. The process is
called cassacao in Brazil. Later Geisel

neatly foiled what appeared to be an
attempted palace coup, making plotting
generals appear before him personally
and reaffirm their loyalty.

Finally, he announced that his
nominee for the presidency was none
other than General João Batista
Figueiredo, head of the Brazilian secret
police, the National Information Services.

Last autumn Geisel feigned per-
plexity: 'One finds it difficult to
understand that there are still those who
express surprise and astonishment at the
rather common expression "relative
democracy".' A few weeks earlier over
1,500 students had been arrested. The
Brazilian press had published reports
of fresh torture – apparently people
have been kept naked in refrigerated

The Brazilian economic miracle

Arrested in São Paulo. Does he have an appointment with the pianola Boilenson?

Tender persuasion

concrete cells deafened by noise for five days at a time.

A São Paulo journalist wrote: 'People are tired of swords and horses. People urinate on heroes' statues.' And he was promptly gaoled. None of this was mentioned when, earlier this year, Prince Charles of England took an all expenses paid tour up the Amazon river. Brazil has 100 million people. It is the tenth largest country on earth. It exports arms throughout the Third World, and is planning soon to have a fully fledged nuclear industry.

At the same time the United States' second largest bank – Citybank – makes more profit from its lendings there than it does in London, banking centre of the world. The Amazon region is now being apportioned to speculators in blocks as large as Holland. The country has a phenomenal thirty-billion-dollar foreign debt. That is the Brazilian economic miracle, on the other side of the national equation 'Security and Development'.

BURUNDI/RWANDA

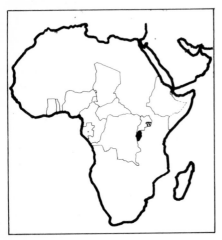

Burundi is the scene of the massacre the world ignored. In six weeks up to 200,000 men, women and children were butchered in an orgy of genocide. In June 1972 even the then President, Michel Micombero, admitted at a press conference that 100,000 had died. The OAU and the UN made no effective protest – even though UNICEF (Children's Fund) jeeps had been used to carry away thousands of corpses to mass graves.

Micombero has since been ousted in a military coup. But all the ingredients are there for the massacre to happen again.

The events of May and June 1972 arose from rivalry between the Tutsi tribe and the Hutus. The small, land-locked, poverty-stricken but beautiful country had been ruled since the sixteenth century by the giant Tutsi (often seven feet tall), along with neighbouring Rawanda, until 1890 when they were occupied by the Germans. Micombero had seized power in one of the frequent military coups which followed independence in 1961, and declared the country a republic.

On 29 April 1972 the Hutu, who made up eighty-four per cent of the population, staged one of their periodic uprisings against their feudal overlords.

Rebels marched into the country with automatics and bows and arrows dipped in poison. An estimated 2,000 Tutsi died in the fighting. Micombero said on the radio there were 'indescribable atrocities. Mothers with babes in arms were massacred. Mothers-to-be were treated so indescribably as to revolt human conscience.'

He then launched the Tutsi reply. On 6 May hundreds of prominent Hutu were 'tried' before 'war councils', executed, and buried in mass graves dug by excavators the same evening. Soon all pretext of courts was abandoned. Random slaughter, in many cases for personal spite or to acquire property, turned to genocide.

A report by the Minority Rights Group in London, published in 1974, pieced together the most definite account of the atrocities, many of which were committed by the '*jeunesses*', youths who went onto the streets crazed with drugs, drink and magic which they thought rendered them invulnerable. Some were shot by the army like rabid dogs. 'The repression took on the qualities of a "selective genocide" directed at all the educated or semi-educated strata of Hutu society.' Groups of soldiers and *jeunesses* appeared in school classrooms and the university in Bujumbura, called the Hutu children by name and took them away: 'Not only the Hutu elites but nearly all potential elites were thus physically liquidated.'

Peasant farmers, shop assistants, gardeners, cooks, nurses – people who could have had no part in the uprising – were murdered in their thousands. 'Arrest warrants' were often forged. 'Those arrested were usually dead the same night, stripped and practically clubbed to death in covered lorries on the way to prison, then finished off with clubs at nightfall. Using bullets would have been wasteful . . .'

Attempted 'breakouts' in the city gaols were dealt with by throwing hand grenades into the cells. One witness said there had been sixty in his cell which measured two metres square. They were piled in layers on top of each other.

The clergy did not escape: 'Twelve Hutu priests are said to have been killed and thousands of Protestant pastors, school directors and teachers.'

Bands of Tutsi combed the country for Hutu, rounding them up into lorries and UNICEF Land-Rovers at gunpoint. Torture, rape, mutilation and wholesale razing of villages followed.

There was practically no protest. The MRG report says: 'As one knowledgeable observer put it: "French military assistants were holding the helicopters steady while Burundi soldiers were machine-gunning Hutu rebels out of the side-windows".' The Belgians, who hold most of the business interests, muttered about sanctions in Brussels, but the threats were not taken seriously. The OAU sent Micombero a message hoping he would resolve the situation quickly; the UN sent a team of five men. It noted its Land-Rovers had been used.

Micombero lasted until November 1976, when he was thrown out by the present ruler, Lieutenant-Colonel Jean-Baptiste Bagaza in a coup.

Throughout he had followed a policy of blind repression towards the Hutu, who have fled in their thousands.

'From the . . . repression a new society has in fact emerged, in which only Tutsi elements are qualified to gain access to power, influence and wealth . . . Hutu status has become synonymous with an inferior category of beings . . . It [Burundi] has become the only state n independent black Africa to claim he appurtenances of a genuine caste ociety; a country in which power is the nonopoly of a dominant ethnic minority epresenting less than fifteen per cent of the total population . . . The pattern of dominance extends to virtually all ectors of life, restricting access to naterial wealth, status and power to epresentatives of the dominant society.'

Bagaza, with five years' training at he Brussels military academy, has announced that he is bent on economic and ocial reform and put four Hutu in his idministration. But he is to a large extent the prisoner of the Tutsi who backed his coup, and the Hutu are expected to rise again.

Rwanda

Rwanda shared the history of Burundi until 1959 when the Hutu rebelled, deposed the Tutsi king, and declared a republic, recognized by the Belgian administration. Government was by an executive president, a council of ministers and a forty-nine-member national assembly until the present ruler, Major-General Juvenal Habyarimana, staged a coup in 1973, replaced the elected government with military officials, and banned all political activities.

In 1964 the Hutu massacred several

President Michel Micombero, who supervised the massacre which the world ignored, with his son Alain
Rex Features

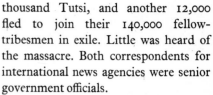

thousand Tutsi, and another 12,000 fled to join their 140,000 fellow-tribesmen in exile. Little was heard of the massacre. Both correspondents for international news agencies were senior government officials.

Like Burundi, Rwanda is one of the poorest countries on earth. With an area of only 10,000 square miles and an estimated population of five million it has the highest population density in Africa. The growth rate is nearly three per cent, only a third of the land is cultivable and another third suitable only for pasture. Ninety-five per cent of the agricultural production is for subsistence, fertilizers are just being heard of, and soil exhaustion is reducing yields. In the fertile volcanic area of the north-west the average family has 1.5 acres to live off. The bamboo and rain forests are practically useless economically and the cash crops of coffee, tea and tin ore at the mercy of wildly fluctuating world market prices.

A massive aid programme from the Belgians, the Common Market Development Fund and the UN continues to supplement the tiny government income.

There is practically no industry or modern development. The latest UN statistics give an infant mortality rate of 132.8 per thousand and a life expectancy at birth of 39.4 (male) and 42.6 (female). There are three cinemas in the entire country, two dentists and one doctor for every 53,506 people.

The country is landlocked and entirely dependent for supplies on routes through Burundi, which has cut them off, or Uganda. Amin has frequently blocked this route, seizing petrol tankers for himself and causing the whole country to grind to a halt.

The military régime is now pinning its faith on tourism (the hilly country is referred to as 'the Switzerland of Belgium'), rich deposits of methane gas and a big hydro-electric potential. Otherwise observers think it is destined for population calamity and rural slumdom.

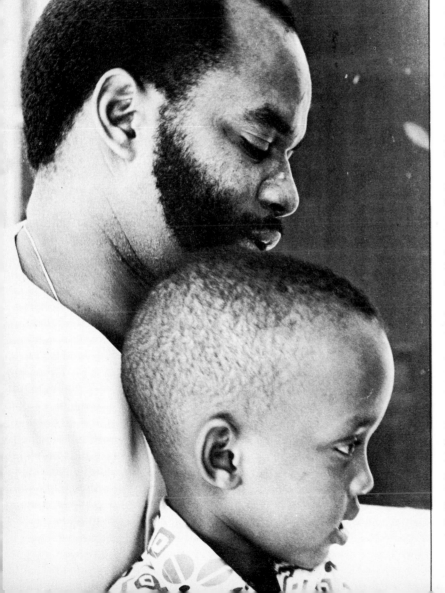

CENTRAL AFRICAN EMPIRE

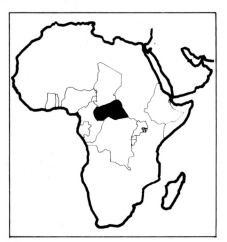

A £3 million display case – Bokassa (quite) triumphant on his tasteless massive throne *Camera Press*

Jean Bedel Bokassa served twenty-three years in the French army, survived the Dien Bien Phu massacre, and was promoted to sergeant. In 1965 he seized power through a military coup in the Central African Republic, shot himself at a dizzy speed through the ranks to Field Marshal, President for Life, Marshal of the Republic, and awarded himself so many medals and decorations that a special apron had to be sewn onto his tunic to accommodate them.

In 1976, following the adoption of an Imperial Constitution, six cabinet reshuffles and his temporary conversion to Islam, he gave himself the ultimate accolade. He turned his country into an Empire and made himself Emperor Bokassa I.

The ludicrous ceremony which followed was modelled on his hero Napoleon and watched in complete amazement by his 2.25 million subjects, officially listed as living in one of the twenty-five poorest nations on earth and ravaged by diseases like river blindness, bilharzia and virulent gonorrhoea. Men can expect to live to thirty-three, women to thirty-six.

'Papa Bok', as they call him, had already been noticed by the outside world for ordering that thieves have their ears cut off and inviting reporters along to watch his soldiers clubbing petty criminals. Three died, dozens were permanently maimed. 'It's tough but that's life,' he said.

In 1971 he was told it was International Women's Year. He promptly freed all the women in Bangui gaol. All the men convicted of crimes against women were executed.

France footed the bill for most of his extravaganza, which cost an estimated £16 million – about half the gross national product – and bankrupted the national exchequer, which he treats as a personal bank account and which has given him a château on the Loire, a fifty-room house in Paris, and an apartment (and numbered account) in Switzerland. Giscard d'Estaing had told him in 1975 that France 'approved his every wish'. Bokassa interpreted this as a licence to print money he did not even have.

His envoys toured France leaving a stream of unpaid bills. Following the Napoleonic theme the Pope was invited to crown him but refused, so he crowned himself. For weeks beforehand he pushed a model of the Imperial coach up and down his palace floor, saying excitedly 'me me me me'. On 4 December the great event took place after he had imported from France 150 tons of wines and cognacs, 400 tons of handcrafted furniture, thirty-five grey Normandy horses (life expectancy in the climate four to five weeks), the Imperial crown (studded with 8,000 diamonds, topped by a solid gold globe of the world and valued at £2.75 million), the Imperial throne (a massive tasteless three-ton

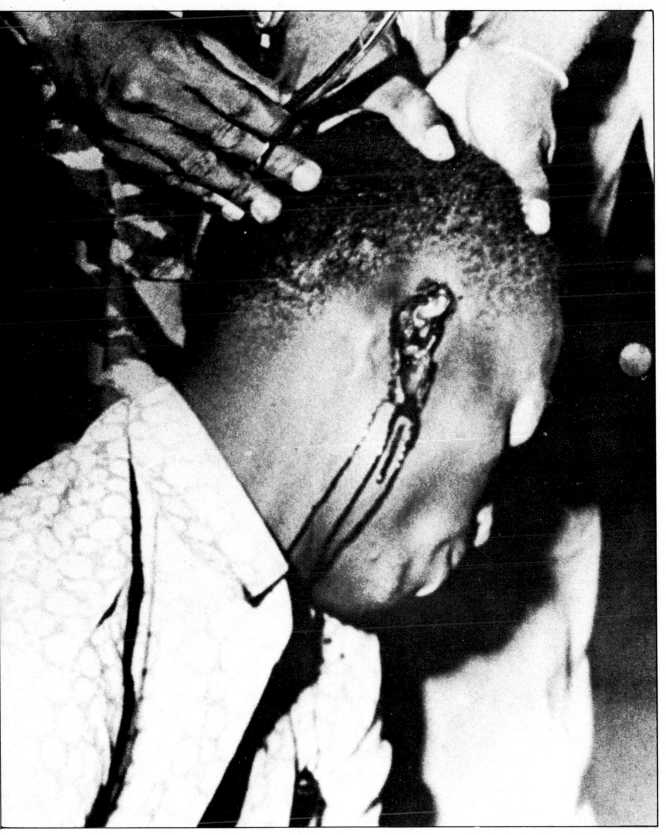

Justice in the Central African Empire
Gamma

Studies in concentration – the Napoleon of Africa enjoying reviewing his subjects *Keystone Press*

monster shaped like an eagle), and four full-sized concrete replicas of the Arc de Triomphe. The Imperial Guard had uniforms tailored by Pierre Cardin, dignitaries travelled in sixty Mercedes limousines, the police on 150 huge BMW motor-cycles, and the natives were ordered 'to break into spontaneous rejoicing in Bangui and the provinces'.

Some countries, appalled, refused to send delegates, others delegated the job to humble minions. Carter cut off US aid in disgust. Bokassa did not care. He dealt with local dissidents, including ministers, by locking them up, and processed into the Coronation room

Justice in the Central African Empire. Pictures put up graphically warning the fate that faces thieves *Gamma*

(an indoor basketball stadium) wearing a Roman toga and a sash in the imperial colours of red, white, blue, green and yellow. The ceremony was accompanied by the mixed strains of Mozart, Beethoven's Ninth, and tribal drums, and only slightly marred by a tip of a coup attempt which led to him leaving by a side-door.

The next day he appeared dressed as an eighteenth-century admiral to review a mixed march-past of 200,000 citizens – a bizarre medley of pygmies, bare-breasted native women dancers, combat-clad assault troops equipped with Soviet weapons, musicians playing four-foot-long treebark trumpets and American-style drum majorettes with white busby hats.

All the world's newspapers were

ordered so he could bask in their admiration. When he read them they were promptly confiscated. Condemnation had been unanimous, but he stays in power, receives twenty-two US dollars a year in multilateral aid for each of his subjects, and still has France to pay his bills. He has prudently retained his French citizenship, and President Giscard D'Estaing enjoys the hunting in the sparsely-populated country.

CHAD

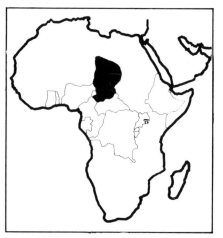

The military government of Chad includes a Secretary of State for Agricultural Development and Natural Disasters. He is needed. The vast semi-desert country was one of the worst sufferers of the Sahel drought. The Deputy Director of Christian Aid described conditions in 1974 as 'horrendous'. The villages in the central provinces reminded him of the Second World War concentration camps with

'Good morning.' General Malloum at his office desk *Camera Press*

the withered limbs and swollen stomachs. There were virtually no drugs or anaesthetics. The hospital in the capital was without even aspirins or bandages.

Millions of pounds in aid have been poured into the country to combat the racking famine but progress has been pitifully slow. In 1977 the FAO granted another 2.5 million US dollars but there is no sign yet of the workable transport system and the huge injections of capital and technical assistance needed. Chad is one of the twenty-five poorest nations on earth, and its financial position so precarious only very soft loans are possible.

Famine is only one of a host of problems for the 4.2 million people. Until 1975 they suffered the bloody and eccentric rule of President Nagarta Tombalbaye who roped in Haitian witch doctors and Stone Age occult ceremonies in his desperate attempts to stay in power. Government officials were made to undergo the ancient secret Yondo ceremony, a form of baptism including frequent beatings, the blood of a tongue ripped from a live chicken, tests of strength like crawling through a termites' nest, and drinking foul concoctions to induce violent vomiting. He had the initiation scars on his own face removed by plastic surgeons in Paris.

At Christmas 1974, paranoid, drinking like a fish and hiding his money in little cardboard boxes, he announced 'the spirit of their ancestors' would speak to the people. It did. 'We, your ancestors, have chosen Nagarta Tombalbaye as your guide,' it said, over the radio. The next April soldiers and police stormed the palace and seized him. Refusing to get on the lorry to take him away he said '*C'est fini*', walked off, and died in a hail of machine-gun fire.

General Felix Malloum Ngakoutou Bey-Ndi was released from prison to head the Supreme Military Council of nine army officers which now rules the country. The constitution was suspended and political parties banned.

Opposite sides. Frolinat rebels being briefed before attacking a desert town *Gamma*

Chad is now in the throes of a civil war for which the former colonial power of France is largely to blame. The French assumed title to all the land, parcelled it out on a concession basis to monopolistic companies, who then looted it and returned practically nothing. The French also incorporated Muslims in the desert north, and black Christians in the south. The Muslims claimed the southerners took over the whole country and have since been fighting to regain it through the guerilla FROLINAT rebels, who now lay claim to two-thirds of the country. France continues to give military and economic assistance, but its position has been complicated by Colonel Qadhafi of Libya, who is backing the rebels and has annexed a chunk of northern territory the size of Scotland on the rumours of rich uranium deposits which could lead him to an independent nuclear capability.

France, with its business interests and a treaty providing for military assistance in the event of a threat to the country, has continued to supply Malloum with help, but at the same time needs to keep good relations with Libya – a good and close supplier of oil and one of the best customers for its arms industry.

Russia has been putting a toe in the water, shipping in some Second World War weapons in 1976, but Malloum has really been looking westwards for support. Carter announced in July 1977 that he was approving a limited military assistance programme. Four American oil companies – Exxon, Shell, Conoco and Chevron – spent twenty-five million dollars on exploration that year. The results have been positive.

The shifting international power struggles have become even more complicated by Sadat worrying in Egypt that Libya might be trying to use the hapless country as the first of a series of

Meanwhile – Chad infantry on foot in the desert with the Foreign Legion get instructions from their Commandant brought in by helicopter *Camera Press*

radical Muslim states designed to stretch across North Africa.

Meanwhile Malloum's government, which executed seven soldiers and two civilians in April 1977 after an attempted coup, has done a little to improve the human rights situation. But this is almost insignificant compared to the urgent need to provide even medieval facilities like wells, to restock the cattle herds virtually wiped out by the drought, and to bring in any modern industry. He can, of course, skim the perks of what proceeds there are from cotton and oil to distribute amongst the elite.

CHILE

only in 1980, and only as a consultative body. One-third of its members will be appointed by Pinochet himself, while the remainder will be appointed by the entire junta. This is reasonable, he said, 'considering the impracticability of elections'. After all, he explained, 'universal vote is an acceptable and adequate method to generate most of the political authorities, yet in itself it cannot magically guarantee success nor always faithfully express the deep will of the nation.' Pinochet alone appreciates what they may be. And to prove it, and further consolidate his personal power within the ruling junta, he called a snap referendum at the beginning of January this year. The other junta members – Gustavo Leigh

Guzmán the Commander-in-Chief of the Air Force, and José Merino Castro the Commander-in-Chief of the Navy, were outraged that Pinochet told them only hours before he broadcast his plans to the nation. The Chilean people had to answer: 'I support President Pinochet in his defence of the dignity of Chile, and I reaffirm the legitimacy of the government . . .'

Leigh and Merino said nobody would respect a plebiscite which the government controlled on a statement like that. But Pinochet, as with all dictators holding referenda, was more interested in achieving the highest possible turn-

'We shall never use a single legal provision to stifle freedom of thought or liberty of conscience, except insofar as to prevent the irresponsible or subversive activity of those who, knowingly or otherwise, could cause us to return to chaos.' – General Pinochet

'The excesses committed by your government in the name of anti-communism are typical of the most tyrannical fascist régimes of our century.'

George Meaney, President of the American AFL-CIO (trade union) to the Chilean Junta, 1977

Augusto Pinochet Ugarte, President of the Republic of Chile, Commander-in-Chief of the Army, has a special mission – to cleanse Chile of all vestiges of parliamentary democracy and replace it with something purer – 'Authoritarian democracy'.

'Authoritarianism does not oppose democracy,' he explains. 'It supplements it by providing it with the necessary means for its subsistence at the service of liberty and the law.' So when the last remaining political party in Chile, the Christian Democrats, looked as if it was pressing to enter the all-military government last year, Pinochet simply decreed the party dissolved. Chile will have a legislative chamber again, but

Body disposal after the coup

ITT's headquarters in New York. They funnelled funds for the CIA, and advocated a military coup to defeat Allende

out. It is at times like this that total government control of the press comes into its own. People were told to go to the polling stations, vote and have their identity cards stamped. If they were not stamped they would be invalid, subject to arrest and denied state benefits. The 'yes' symbol on the voting paper was a large Chilean flag. The 'no' symbol was a black box, ostensibly to help illiterates. Voters noticed they could see through their ballots, while the security forces were being extremely conscientious in supervising the poll. Pinochet announced he had received a seventy-seven per cent vote of 'Yes' – there is no way to prove him wrong – then immediately declared that there would be no more elections in Chile for the next ten years. Such is Chile today, five years after Pinochet's army invaded Santiago, the capital, bombed the presidential palace and began systematically torturing and exterminating the people who worked for Salvador Allende's elected government. The sewers are no longer choked with corpses as they were then. Simply, nearly everyone in the country, at least 30,000 people, whom the government violently opposed, have already been killed. Allende's Minister of Defence, General Pratz, was killed by a bomb in Buenos Aires. His Foreign Minister, Orlando Letelier, was blown up with a car-bomb in Washington. Allende's daughter, Beatrice, took her own life in Havana. A staggering tenth of the population, over a million Chileans, have emigrated rather than live under Pinochet's purified régime. At the time Henry Kissinger said: 'It has become necessary to save the Chilean people from their own mistakes.'

Looking back on his achievements, Pinochet assumes a less callous, slightly more mystical tone. 'When the September 11 breezes once again fill the skies of

our Nation with their mark of Chilean-hood, of triumph and hope, every father or mother must see in the eyes of their children the satisfaction that involves giving them a free existence and real possibilities of a promising future . . .'

That very much depends. Santiago's shops are bursting as never before with imported televisions, hi-fis, automobiles, Paris fashions, whisky and American cigarettes. Last year several entrepreneurs had quickly to flee the country after precipitating a financial collapse by buying up what were government industries on unsecured loans. The multi-nationals are now extracting copper and nitrates, unhampered, at rock bottom prices, and carving up the

The coup. Bombing Salvador Allende in the Presidential Palace

Chilian soldiers paying their respects to General Pinochet, Independence Day Parade

country's prospective off-shore oil reserves. Chile now buys sophisticated weapons from Israel in the face of other countries' arms embargoes.

But the minimum monthly wage, rigidly enforced, buys only enough food to feed the average family for three weeks. Unemployment hovers between fifteen and twenty per cent. And child malnutrition has gone up by half since the coup, largely because parents have no work.

Pinochet occasionally talks to government-appointed union leaders. But he leaves social problems largely to Lucia, 'my dear wife, whose untiring dedication to serving the humblest, strengthens my inner vim'.

As unedifying as it may seem, the Pinochets' domestic life may provide a key to the General's dreams. *El Presidente*, apparently, likes to pee standing up, against a men's urinal, as befits his military bearing. But Lucia

Santiago stadium. Where Victor Jara, the guitarist, had his hands broken before being tortured to death

48

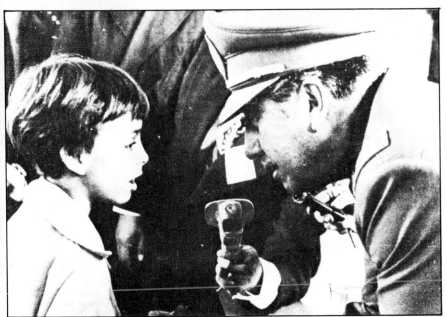

took offence. So in their new opulent mansion they now have three new urinals, especially designed and commissioned to fit in with the other décor. *El Presidente* can pee as he sees fit. The first lady is content.

In the streets of Santiago no one may dare protest. Meanwhile, Eduardo Frei, the head of the Christian Democratic Party, who paved the way to Pinochet's coup by passing a motion in the Chilean parliament declaring Allende's government unconstitutional, tours European capitals soliciting support for a return to civilian rule.

General Pinochet discussing the future of the nation

Pinochet rallies the support of the
middle classes. But one million have
left to live abroad

'On September 11, 1973 the Armed
and Order Forces complied with their
promise to the Nation' – General
Augusto Pinochet

One way to leave the office. The Junta
sorting out the staff they disapprove of

EL SALVADOR

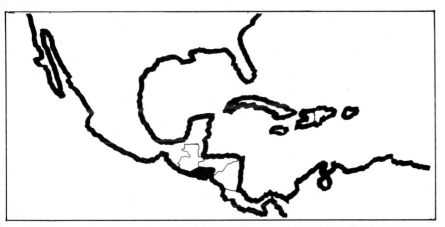

General Carlos Humberto Romero is president of El Salvador because of massive electoral fraud. On 20 February 1977 – polling day – the radio station of the National Water Authority was commandeered by his party, the National Coalition Party, and ORDEN (the Salvadorean anti-communist terror squad which Romero controlled) to broadcast instructions to gangs stuffing ballot boxes. 'Put some *Tamales* in the tank' meant stuff more fraudulent ballots in the boxes.

'Coffee', in the bizarre Water Authority radio broadcast code, meant votes for the opposition. 'Sugar' meant votes for Romero. 'Little birds' were voting inspectors, who occasionally had to be 'given lessons', which meant roughing them up. Dead people were signed on the voting list, which was increased by 300,000 names. The Central Election Board prestamped voting papers which were supposed to be stamped only at the polls. The National University was closed. Opposition organizers were kidnapped and tortured with electric shocks. The army was mobilized in barracks, and the police, doubled in number, intensively patrolled the streets. It took a week for the army to smother the immediate general strike and protests that followed. Factories were burned, schools closed and the main towns paralysed by demonstrations of more than 50,000 irate citizens.

Finally, a state of siege was declared. The security forces opened fire on 2,000 people late at night in San Salvador's (the capital's) main square – Plaza Liberdad. The people fled into a church, where they were choked out with tear-gas grenades. Over one hundred men and women were injured before the Red Cross negotiated a truce.

General Romero. All smiles after having usurped his superiors and exiled his opponents. He likes horse-riding at the San Salvador Jockey Club

This is the only photograph we have. Hope is what you need.

With the Compliments
of the
Embassy of El Salvador

16 EDINBURGH HOUSE
9b PORTLAND PLACE
LONDON W.1. ENGLAND   TELEPHONE: 01 - 636 9563

Officially eight died. Witnesses say it was more like forty. Romero blamed 'agents of communist subversion' who 'drugged people to incite violence'. He also gave the opposition candidate, Colonel Ernesto Claramount, a choice – house arrest, military prison or exile. Claramount fled to neighbouring Costa Rica, the only semi-democratic haven in Central America.

Romero is in power on behalf of the country's businessmen and large landowners. His first act was to throw out piecemeal land reforms which for the first time in over a decade held out some hope for the country's four million peasants and their families.

El Salvador is the smallest and most densely populated country in Central America. It depends for half its income on coffee shipped to West Germany and the United States. Even though a quarter of a million tourists go there each year to lie on its beautiful Pacific beaches, over seventy per cent of the young children suffer from malnutrition, it has the lowest caloric intake per capita in Latin America, and half the able-bodied adults are without jobs or working part time.

Romero is also the United States' man. Trained by them, as Minister of Defence and Public Security between 1972 and 1976 – when he controlled the police, army and ORDEN terrorists. In 1974 farmers were massacred. In 1975, it was the students' turn – at least twenty died and as many again 'disappeared'. He was president of the *Consejo de Defensa Centroamericana*, the regional alliance between the Mexican border and the Panama Canal set up by the United States to co-ordinate the armies they equip, train and maintain. Romero arranged the wholesale purchase of a Salvadoranian air-force, complete with twenty-four jet fighters from Israel and the United States which the country might, possibly, have enough trained pilots to fly. While he profited from military procurements, others did not. Many of El Salvador's officers believe Romero was intimately involved in the arrest and subsequent conviction of his then Chief of Staff, in connection with an attempt to sell 10,000 machine-guns to the American Mafia. Romero was promoted to general within a few months of his boss's arrest. And the president, Romero's predecessor, was passed over and retired from the army's active list. Only Colonel Claramount, Romero's opponent in the '*Tamales*' election fraud, dared publicly challenge his record, pointing out that when El Salvador was at war with Honduras in 1969, Romero was noticeably absent from the front.

El Presidente's reputation comes more from giving riding lessons to the country's debutantes at San Salvador's exclusive Jockey Club. Whether they admire Romero's methods is not known.

Following the '*Tamales*' affair, a pogrom was unleashed against priests, particularly Jesuits who had been helping the peasants. At least seven have been deported, three beaten and tortured, three imprisoned and six murdered, mostly by government troops. A secret terrorist gang, called the 'White Warrior Union', openly demanded the remaining Jesuits in the country be expelled. The Archbishop and all his bishops boycotted Romero's inauguration. Since then, well-documented reports have been made of soldiers and ORDEN members descending on towns, ransacking homes and taking prisoners who subsequently 'disappear', as well as a systematic campaign against trade unionists.

Occasionally left-wing guerilla groups punctuate the scene with a kidnapping or killing. Nonetheless El Salvador has been bending further under the General's control.

EQUATORIAL GUINEA

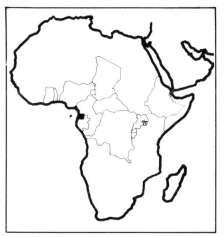

Equatorial Guinea has become today's centre for the slave trade. Twenty thousand of its subjects have been frog-marched from their homes on the African mainland, jammed into boats, and taken to an island over one hundred miles away where they are forced to work as unpaid labour on cocoa plantations.

The island is called Macias Nguema Biyogo after the ruler of the country, Francisco Macias Nguema Biyogo Negue Ndong, President for Life, Major-General of the Armed Forces and Great Maestro of Popular Education, Science and Traditional Culture. He has described himself as 'the only miracle' of the country.

Macias lives in a palace behind a military compound wall that severs the main square of the capital. No one is allowed in without a permit. They are only allowed on the beach if they pay 1,500 pesetas. This means they cannot escape and the fishing industry has collapsed.

Even so, an estimated half of the 400,000 population now live in exile after fleeing, mostly from the mainland province of Rio Muni (now renamed Mbini). They have told a series of stories of systematic torture and extermination. The stories cannot be verified because Macias has turned his island into a hermit country. Journalists and human rights groups are banned, foreign travel restricted and mail censored. Only recently has the extent of the tyranny begun to be exposed. Amnesty International reported in 1976: 'Torture, massacres of civilians and government-sanctioned murder of political opponents had proceeded unchecked to the extent that they are now commonplace.'

Macias took over the country in 1968 after independence granted by Spain, the colonial power which ruled from 1817 when it swopped it with Portugal for a lump of Brazil.

Six months later there was an attempted coup by the foreign minister. Macias armed his youth movement, sent them out on the streets and whipped up hysterical anti-white feeling on the government radio. The 260 *Guardias Civiles* were called out to protect the Spanish residents who fled in terror. Within days the European population had dwindled from its peak of 8,000 to a few hundred.

The foreign minister officially died when he was caught in the palace and jumped out of the window. Refugees said the President's bodyguard broke both his legs with their rifle-butts and tossed him to the mob, who lynched him. His wife was publicly tortured and killed. The country's first ambassador to the United Nations, who had been there for four months, was recalled for 'urgent consultations', accused of being an accomplice, taken behind a bush and summarily executed at the airport.

Other 'criminals' were dealt with differently. On Christmas Eve 1969 a group of 'murderers' were publicly tried in the Fernando Po Peace Football stadium. The spectators were invited to endorse the guilty verdicts. The men were then alternately hung and shot with the pop record 'Those Were the Days' sung by Mary Hopkin blaring out of the loud-speaker system.

But Macias' main target has been his political opponents and intellectuals whom he has described as 'the greatest problem facing Africa today . . . polluting our climate with foreign culture.'

Suzanne Cronjé, in a report for the Anti-Slavery Society in 1976, said: 'Macias has made a clean sweep of almost all Equatorial Guinea's educated classes . . . By the end of 1974 more than two-thirds of the members of the 1968 National Assembly had "disappeared".'

The former deputy president died of thirst in prison, a founder of the Bubi tribe union (Macias belongs to the Fang tribe) died of gangrene after having his eyes gouged out.

The former health minister, now escaped to Cameroon, has told how he watched 157 political dissidents being clubbed to death. A prominent businessman says he was summoned to the presidential palace and ordered to pay Macias £7,000. He had twenty-four hours to raise the money. He collected it, handed it over, and was thrown into gaol, where he stayed for two years. He watched clubbings, beatings with bundles of sticks, and important political prisoners having their tendons cut so they could not escape. Prisoners were made to stand up to their necks in filthy mud and water for twenty-four hours, and forced to eat mouthfuls of red-hot peppers. 'Drink your coffee,' the guards would say, laughing. Prisoners had to club each other for the guards' amusement. In two months the businessman watched sixty-nine people die. One was the former governor of the National Bank. His name still appears on the bank-notes.

In June 1974 Macias announced a

'coup plot' by 114 prisoners in gaol. Large numbers of them were said in the government newspaper to have 'committed suicide' when the plot was uncovered. Before they killed themselves they found time to make lengthy confessions, subsequently quoted verbatim at the military tribunal which judged them posthumously a fortnight later.

In December 1974 the World Council of Churches denounced Macias as 'a modern Caligula' and his country as a vast concentration camp. Priests had joined the businessmen, civil servants, administrators and teachers who were systematically tortured and executed. Catholic schools have been outlawed, 'priests and pastors' forbidden to travel inside the country or abroad, Mass banned, sermons censored beforehand, and nuns and priests arrested for refusing to read Macias' praise during services.

Macias' paranoia has been unalleviated by the hysterical chants of 'We march with Macias. Always with Macias. Nothing without Macias' which greet his public appearances. Refugees report the population as living in terror and 'hopeless resignation'.

The ordinary people have not escaped. The Anti-Slavery Society report says: 'The catalogue of death concentrates only on the best-known political leaders and says nothing of the hundreds of men, women and children who were unknown outside their country when they met similar fates. In many cases people have been punished or executed without even a pretence that they were guilty of a crime . . . in some cases whole villages have been destroyed when a member of the community was accused of disloyalty to Macias or some such crime.'

Meanwhile his island has been collapsing into chaos. A UN Development Programme pamphlet published in August 1975 as an internal guide for personnel stated 'Malaria, fiariasas, infectious hepatitis, dysentery and whooping cough are endemic throughout Equatorial Guinea. Tuberculosis and parasitic intestinal diseases prevail.' Medicine and drugs are virtually unobtainable: 'All basic foodstuffs must be imported as no fresh or preserved meat, poultry, eggs, butter, cheese, rice, milk, flour is available.'

Refugees have reported the economy in ruins, the shops empty, the roads a mass of potholes, practically no local transport, and the electricity supply constantly breaking down for weeks at a time.

Macias has been made President for Life by the sole political party, PUNT. In a rare interview with the BBC he said: 'We train the children so that we can have their minds according to our party.' His military youth movement recruits from the age of seven upwards. By Presidential decree in 1976, supported by PUNT, he reintroduced slavery.

His island economy has always depended on cocoa, harvested by Nigerian labourers under a formal agreement signed in 1942. In 1976 the

A brief excursion from his enclave. President Macias Nguema of Equatorial Guinea reviewing troops of the Nigerians, who used to provide his contract labour *Camera Press*

Nigerians finally evacuated the last of the 45,000 labourers, accusing Macias' government and employers of 'barbaric treatment'. In 1971 ninety-five were shot for demanding arrears of wages. The brutality culminated in troops opening fire on the last refugee ship, killing three.

With no workers Macias turned to Mbini, his mainland province, for salvation. The guards in each of the ten regions were ordered to arrest between 2,000 and 2,500 people, who were then taken to the island to work as forced labour on the crumbling plantations. Refugees say they are still there today, working as unpaid forced labour.

According to Western sources Macias' tyranny is supported by Cuban, Chinese and Russian experts. His régime is theoretically Marxist. In March 1976

David Ennals, Britain's Minister of State for Foreign Affairs, told Parliament that Cuban soldiers were being used 'in advisory and training roles'. In September 1977 he went to Peking.

But he has had Western help. French companies have been involved in modernizing Bata harbour and a French company built his administrative complex.

Until recently Spaniards were forbidden to know about Equatorial Guinea under the *materia reservada* law, which prohibited publication of any information in the media. The Spanish government has signed contracts to buy Macias' cocoa (reputedly the best in the world) at higher than market prices, supplied experts to run the state airline, and given its national telephone company, CTNE, the job of supplying personnel to keep the system running.

'Appreciable budget assistance' has been given along with 'cultural aid'.

But in March 1977 diplomatic relations were officially severed after Macias publicly insulted Juan Carlos in a speech. However, Macias is said to connive with absentee plantation owners and businessmen using natives as fronts.

Other African countries, whilst condemning Amin, have made little protest about him. The UN's Human Rights Sub-Commission on Prevention of Discrimination and Protection of Minorities rejected a report in March 1976. One delegate was reported afterwards as saying it was 'horrifying', but had been dismissed because it was prepared by refugees, and investigators were refused permission to enter the country.

A National Alliance for the Restoration of Democracy in Equatorial Guinea has now announced in Spain that it is gathering forces for an armed invasion to overthrow Macias.

In February 1978 his wife was said to have fled the country, and in a fit of pique he has now made it an offence for any baby to be baptised with her name – Monica.

ETHIOPIA & SOMALIA

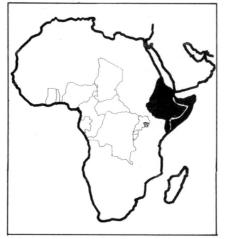

The intervention of President Carter in March 1978 put a temporary end to the festering border dispute between these two enormous desert countries. Refugees – their total number expected to run into hundreds of thousands – poured into the Somali Democratic Republic – their camels dead, their collapsible tents of hides and sticks destroyed and their nomadic life over. The Russian and Cuban mechanized columns of the advancing Ethiopian

Ethiopia. Waiting for food distribution at a relief camp

army were accused of wholesale and indiscriminate slaughter with their modern weapons – Russian T-55 tanks, Kalashnikovs and air strikes with modern jet fighters.

The tenseness between the superpowers over the battle for the strategic importance of the area – the Horn of Africa which can control the vital oil supply route for the West – evaporated for a period. It is expected to return.

Meanwhile the respective Marxist governments have been left to concentrate on their own problems, which are in both cases enormous. The inhabitants of Somalia are infinitely better off. In 1976 the Somali Revolutionary Socialist Party was established to take over the functions of the

Red terror and White terror, Addis Ababa. Early morning street scene with corpses left as an example to those 'opposing' the revolution *Gamma*

military Supreme Revolutionary Council, which threw out the civilian government in 1969. Brigadier Siyad Barre is now President, and Amnesty International, through adopting them as prisoners of conscience, has been trying to get something done about the unknown number of people detained in solitary confinement for their opposition to the régime. The régime has denied it tortured foreigners shipwrecked on the barren coastline.

It is in Ethiopia that the hapless people have had to suffer the iron rule and bloody infighting which has led to at least 30,000 murders in the past four years. Until 1974 the twenty-eight

Ethiopia. Undernourishment and fatalism

million population had lived under the corrupt, brutal and inefficient rule of Emperor Haile Selassie, the largest recipient of US aid in Africa during the fifties and sixties. Keeping his peasants in virtual feudalism, his executions, arbitrary and long-term detention of political prisoners and torture he changed to vague promises of land reform and even two pay rises for the army to try to stop the mounting tide of discontent. It was no use. The Provisional Military Administration Council, the Dergue, threw him out in a coup and the wizened little old man died shortly afterwards in mysterious circumstances.

Whatever rejoicing followed his overthrow was short-lived. Since then Lieutenant-Colonel Mengistu Haile Mariam has presided over the bloodiest period in the ancient country's history. The war with Somalia, important though it may have been to outsiders, has been nothing compared to the massacres which have taken place through the twin factors of the Eritrean secessionist war, and the ruthless fighting between the two rival groups vying with each other for leadership of the scientific socialist revolution – exemplified by the renaming of the main square in Addis Ababa as 'Red Square' and the giant posters of Marx and Lenin, floodlit at night when the electricity supply is working.

Mengistu, five years ago, was an obscure army major, now ironically converted to passionate ideological belief through his close contacts with the Marxist students whom he is busy decimating. For once there has been no need for foreign correspondents to invent the slaughter which the hacks bashed out in Ishmaelia in Evelyn Waugh's book, *Scoop*.

Mengistu has been ordering murder on three fronts – his genuine and

Ethiopia. Walk if you can. Old man trying to reach relief camp during the famine in the Wollo province

Somalia – the bosses

imagined political opponents; the genu
ine and supposed supporters of th
fight for the secession of Eritrea, th
Northern seaboard province annexed b
Selassie in the early sixties; and final
through the Somalian war. His extra
ordinary bent for power and violence
said by some to hark back to his origi
of belonging to the lowest ethnic orde
the old 'slave tribe'.

Whatever the reason, nobody is saf
from the highest to the lowest. The 12
members of the Dergue have bee
reduced, in two years, to sixty through
series of executions, the most systemat
being in February 1977, when seventee
died, including the Head of State. T
next day he gathered together 100,00
to approve his actions in a mass rally.

The power struggle is between hi
and the members of the politburea
wanting a civilian Marxist governmen
who see his side as a crypto-sociali
bloody dictatorship. It has pitte
civilians against soldiers, and socialis
against nationalism and led to bot

Ethiopia – carrying the precious water

The President at the mike. Listen carefully

...ides arming their supporters. The result has been the series of assassinations by the rival gangs of the Red Terror (pro government) and White Terror (anti). Both groups roam the streets of the capital murdering on the slightest pretext. Mengistu put his supporters on the streets in 1977 saying that the country had reached the point where anarchy, sabotage and subversion could no longer be tolerated. He called on Ethiopians to 'wield the revolutionary hammer against those who seek to dismember the nation'. They have. On 19 December 1977 the bodies of 300 'counter-revolutionaries' were publicly displayed on the streets, after they had been murdered.

The purge of 'counter-revolutionary' members leaves bodies lying on the streets night after night, with notes pinned to their backs like: 'This is a revenge measure. We are tired of burying counter-revolutionaries.'

Civilians have been backed up by the army, particularly the 'Flame' Brigade, formed to suppress dissent. Intellectuals have been the main target, and foreigners who have visited the country have reported dozens of massacres and atrocities. Students have been killed in their thousands, children jammed into trucks, ordered at gunpoint to help dig their own graves and then machine-gunned by the assassination squads. Mengistu's switch of alliance from American support for his country (the US trained 20,000 troops for Selassie) to the Russians and Cubans has made no difference, and the atrocities in the political infighting have been paralleled in the Eritrea war, with bodies of children left in piles by the roadside for the hyenas, and random killings by peasant associations rather than the workers in the urban centres. In Eritrea the murder squad is called 'The Stranglers'.

More cruel ironies have emerged. War on Want reported that the Eritreans desperately needed medicines for the 5,000 disease-stricken government soldiers they had captured and were keeping in concentration camps. The government of course denied that the camps existed.

Mengistu has had constant problems with his soldiers, press-ganged and forced to the front after a month's rough training, who often abandon their Kalashnikovs unfired. Wholesale desertion has been answered with execution by firing squad, and he has rushed round his various fronts trying to boost flagging morale. In January 1978 his reply on the Ogaden front was a bomb thrown at him which killed six of his officers. Mutinies have been followed by frequent purges of all ranks. The executions are often described as the victims being 'subjected to a counter-revolutionary measure'.

This bloodshed has temporarily distracted from the other horrors shared by both countries – their sheer poverty. Ethiopia's fast-growing population is now thought to be heading rapidly for ecological disaster due to massive soil erosion and deforestation. The civil service is paralysed, partly due to the indoctrination programme which involves compulsory political meetings every Monday and Friday afternoon. The country is a logistical nightmare, with fourteen million of the population living twenty miles from the nearest road. If the food they grow can get to the road, convoys to bring it to the cities have to be under military escort because of guerillas; two-thirds of the trucks are now out of action because of a lack of spare parts and ferocious driving; and when the rains come everything turns into a sea of mud. The rains do not come often enough, which is another major problem. In 1977 it was announced that forty million dollars' worth of crops had been left to rot in the fields, but the main difficulty has been the drought which has affected both countries.

Over 400,000 people are estimated to have died in the droughts towards the end of Selassie's régime, which was not revealed to the outside world until years after they had started. What has been grown since in the vast country – almost as large as Western Europe – has not only had to cope with the weather but with the imposition of co-operative farms on peasants who were barely emerging from feudalism. The farms in Ethiopia have been a complete failure.

In Somalia the series of 'crash programmes' instituted by the military régime have been more successful, the

Somalia – crash programme volunteers
(with entrenching tools)

independent people enthusiastically welcoming a massive series of aid projects, ranging from malaria eradication to the construction of hospitals and processing plants. China, the UN, the WHO, and the Western nations have combined to help with jobs, including tracking down isolated cases of smallpox. The West Germans, in thanks for assistance in the Mogadishu raid, are now helping the Chinese to dig wells. Not all projects have worked. The Americans some time ago built a fish and lobster processing plant which could handle forty tons a day. The local fishermen in their dhows took six months to catch that amount. The government was left with repair and running costs for the plant. Highly expensive canneries have often operated at half capacity, if that; ten million US dollars' worth of aid has been wiped out by the Ogaden war. Political problems have only added to the difficulties. The Russians, before Barre booted them out and they went to help the Ethiopians, had set up a venture to create a national fishing fleet. When they were expelled they sailed off in their trawlers, dumping the native crews. The whole thing collapsed overnight. It had been little use anyhow. The Russians had insisted that the project be paid for by the produce, which meant that the cans of fish were taken back home for Soviet citizens to buy in their shops.

In Ethiopia on the state farms there have been technical difficulties, labour troubles, and bottle-necks due to lack of spare parts. The Government has insisted that rehabilitation work should have equal priority with land redistribution, and Western projects be redesigned on 'socialist' lines.

In 1976 out of a cumulative total of 658 million dollars aid committed, some dating back several years, only seventy-four millions was spent.

It is now thought that there is a dead-line fast approaching. In five or ten years the ecological decline will be irreversible – except by methods the country cannot afford – and will lead to what has been described as the world's first 'superfamine'.

Prospects in Somalia are thought to be brighter because the people can genuinely help each other, but at the same time the country has suffered a massive drain of skilled personnel to the Gulf region, where the rich Arab states pay them ten times the salary they can expect in Mogadishu.

Somalia. Not a riot but the ceremonial New Year stick game at Afghoi. The size of the sticks is now controlled for safety

If you can't get the real thing. May Day
celebrations with wooden rifles in
Addis Ababa *Gamma*

GABON

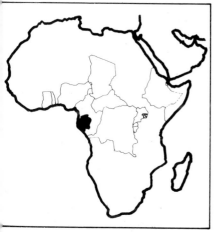

His Excellency El Hadj Omar Bongo, President of the République Gabonaise, is neither a tyrant nor a military dictator. But he deserves a special prize for his mindless extravagance, the inequality with which he distributes his country's wealth, and his close collaboration with his country's former rulers – the French.

Bongo inherited Gabon from the late Leon M'Ba, whom de Gaulle restored to power with a posse of French paratroopers in 1964. He is now seeking to reduce his economic dependence on the French and in 1977 was the first African leader to be received by Carter. He has had diplomatic relations with Russia and China.

But he and the French are still doing good business. In 1977 there were an estimated 30,000 French citizens living in the country and total French investment of £700 million.

Bongo has long since released the political opponents he gaoled when he took over in 1967 and has given them lucrative posts in government or the political party. Relatives hold strategic positions in the army.

The result has been a beano for everybody except the majority of the tiny population, thought to be less than one million.

Gabon is bursting with natural re-

Women working the fields away from the £165 million palace

Maintaining the French Connection – Bongo and family in the snow of the Alpes Maritimes *Keystone Press*

sources. Its iron-ore deposits are being gouged out by a consortium of French banks, German companies and the American giant, Bethlehem Steel. Oil flows in from the off-shore wells and moderate taxes are paid in return. The forests yield hardwoods and a near-world monopoly of Okoume, for the finest quality plywood (which is also blamed for the legendary sterility of Gabonese women). The French Atomic Energy Commission is happily prising out the vast uranium deposits.

And Bongo has been spending, mostly, of course, in France. He owns a futuristic £165 million palace with acres of marble, lashings of gold fittings, and dozens of automatic doors which glide open at a touch of the Cuban heels he wears to disguise his diminutive stature.

His most astonishing exploit so far has been the fourteenth annual summit meeting of the Organization of African Unity, which took place in the capital, Libreville, in July 1977. The cost of the ten-day meeting, supposedly to discuss serious politics, is reckoned at £350 million – half Gabon's gross national product.

Rows of gleaming hotels were built on the sea-front and a three-mile-long dual carriageway laid to connect them with the enormous conference centre, theatre, banqueting hall and fifty presidential chalets.

Transport was seen to by the import of two £70,000 replicas of the armour-plated American presidential machine, six secret service Cadillacs, fifty Mercedes limousines, 100 of the latest Peugeots and 300 BMW motor-cycles. Processions were trailed by a new presidential ambulance in case of emergencies.

Overnight Libreville overtook Caracas to become the most expensive city in the world, with hapless non-delegates paying £7 or more to eat revolting simple meals and forking out extortionate sums for hire cars which had been commandeered by the government.

The delegates themselves, drinking some of the finest French wines out of the 10,000 hand-cut crystal glasses, could admire the special weather-proof posters, imported from Paris, which proclaimed 'Africa is for the Africans'.

But most were not happy. The French were entrusted with the security arrange-

ments, and descended on the airport with such a battery of complicated electronic apparatus that the Malaw delegation – for example – struggled for nine hours to gain entry to the country and the hotel rooms which were the only alternative to shacking up in the nearby slums.

They soon became unanimous in condemning such money-minded in efficiency. The last straw came in two ways. During the ten days there was no laundry service in any of the hotels. The laundry workers had been transformed into gaily-dressed cheer groups bundled out into the streets, and ordered to break into spontaneous rejoicing whenever Bongo appeared. They would not be back at work until the conference was over.

And there were no Gabonese ladies in the nightclubs. They were at home faithfully following the presidential decree not to 'fraternize' with the delegates.

It was, the Tanzanian delegate was quoted as saying, 'capitalism and neo colonialism gone mad'.

Gabon was where Albert Schweitzer set up his leper hospital.

GHANA

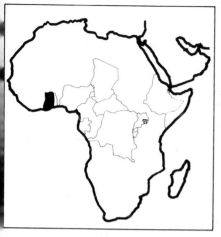

General Acheampong. Cowboy movies now. Civilian clothes later?

General Ignatius K. Acheampong made a promise when he took over Ghana with a military coup on 13 January 1972: 'As soon as circumstances permit we shall hand over to a democratically elected government.'

His military régime has now been in power for longer than any other government since the British granted their former colony of the Gold Coast independence in 1957.

But a series of strikes by professional organizations and demonstrations by students have now forced him to agree to a leisurely time-table to fulfil his promise. If all goes smoothly the military will bow out on 1 July 1979.

Until then Acheampong intends to continue with the present government. He is Head of State, Head of the Supreme Military Council, Chairman of the National Redemption Council and Minister of Defence, Finance and Cocoa Affairs. The SMC, the highest legislative and administrative body, is chaired by him and made up of the Chief of Defence Staff, the Army Commander, the Navy Commander, the Border Guards Commander and the Inspector-General of Police. The secondary body, the NRC, again has Acheampong in the chair, and is composed of members who hold office by virtue of their service or government appointments, as do the nine regional commissioners, who are all army officers.

Ghana has alternately veered between civilian and military government over the past twenty-one years, with the previous longest stayer being the notorious Dr Kwame Nkrumah, the great white hope of the liberals. Nkrumah hung on for six years after proclaiming Ghana a republic in 1960, moving further and further east in his politics until he was ousted by the military while he was enjoying a hero's reception in Peking. He touted around looking for a chance of a come-back until April 1973, when he died in exile. Three months later his body was flown back for burial at his birthplace, a posthumous propaganda campaign resurrected him as 'a great leader', and Acheampong's government finally sorted out the tangle of the great 'Nkrumah debt' he left behind with a promise of repayment over twenty-eight years.

The changes have been mainly due to the complications of the country. The south has a hideously humid climate, with two annual rainfalls totalling anything up to seven feet, while the north peters out into scrub and savannah. The people divide into four main groups, and speak seventy-five different languages and dialects. The official one is English.

The economy is based almost entirely on cocoa, imported by an African blacksmith in 1879. Acheampong, putting the country on the 'pragmatic nationalism' road, has borrowed large

1966. Nkrumah goes. The people are now taught that he was a great leader

Modern estates in the capital Accra

amounts, mostly interest-free, from the US, Britain and other Western nations while the Chinese and Russians provide technical and financial help.

A keen churchman ('I believe in God and nothing without Him') and cowboy movie addict, he has been urging his 9.6 million population to end Ghana's reliance on food imports with a Charter of Redemption, exhorting patriotism, moral improvement and his 'Seven Principles', a policy of 'Self Reliance' and a crash programme entitled 'Operation Feed Yourself'.

The two-thirds of his people who are engaged in subsistence agriculture have so far responded with the indifference with which they greeted his coup, seeming to prefer banana beer. Efforts to build up an independent economy have not yet succeeded.

In 1975 a combination of a bad harvest, higher import prices and the reliance on deficit financing forced the national consumer price index up by thirty per cent. It rose by sixty per cent the following year, when drought led to a flood of free grain from the United States, Canada and Europe – until the US suspended its shipments because of the vast corruption.

The sale of the free grain and sorghum was blatant and widespread. Acheampong, at a press conference in January 1978, shifted the blame to the local paramount chiefs, whom he said were an important part of the administration, and the Catholic church, which he alleged had used supplies to blackmail local tribesmen into becoming Catholics. Priests admitted that, with no organization, they had had to distribute food informally, but gave examples of how district officials had utilized the famine. One allegedly got his hands on 200 tons of American sorghum and sold it to the poverty-stricken people at the height of the crisis for six US dollars a bowl.

Acheampong has promised it will not happen again. Officials have been fired and a new emergency relief network set up.

Meanwhile this military man, trained at the staff college at Fort Leavenworth, Kansas, has been having his main trouble with his educated civilians.

A coup attempt was easily dealt with by a batch of death sentences (later commuted to life imprisonment) for the conspirators, some of whom alleged at their trial that they had been tortured. The British legal system has been neatly got round by the Subversion Decree of 1976, which makes the decisions of military tribunals immune from challenge in other courts of law.

But in June and July 1977 a political strike by doctors, lawyers, engineers and students successfully crystallized opposition and paralysed the country.

Acheampong gave in with the promise of 'union government' by means of a referendum, a draft constitution drawn up by a commission and then ratified, and finally civilian rule.

The system of government will be similar to the American one, except that there will be no parties. Which has led some people to ask how it will work, especially as it will not be explained to the people before the referendum. They simply vote 'union government – yes' or 'union government – no' by tearing off the appropriate side of a perforated piece of paper and putting it in the ballot box. The other goes into a vat of acid, to prevent fraud.

The professionals have also been finding life hard. The President of the Ghana Bar Association now owns a burnt-out wreck which was his Mercedes, piles of abusive mail have arrived at various homes, and a meeting to discuss 'union government' on 12 October 1977 was wrecked by a crowd of thugs.

Acheampong, known for his lack of personal charisma but respected for his keen sense of timing and grasp of politics, has naturally condemned the violence. And he does not seem averse to running for the civilian presidency himself. In autumn 1977 he said: 'If the people whom I represent today as Head of State and Chairman of the Supreme Military Council decided to nominate me as a presidential candidate, fine – I may have to consider such an offer on its merits.'

With his propaganda machine and the absence of any political parties he is expected to start as odds-on favourite if he enters the race, and continue in power – as plain Mr Acheampong.

GUATEMALA

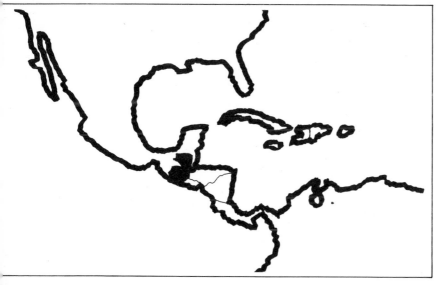

Guatemala supposedly is changing. Visitors report fewer men in Guatemala City with six-shooters strapped to their thighs. The preference now seems to be for smaller, lighter automatic pistols which slip into pockets.

With possibilities of oil deposits estimated by some American geologists to rival even those of Saudi Arabia, the country's 5.5 million people could reasonably expect the infant mortality rate – which is by far the worst in Central America – rapidly to fall, the malnutrition which afflicts four out of five children under five virtually to disappear, and the minimum wage, which now stands at 1.42 dollars a day, to be tripled, or at least doubled over-

People live on hillsides because all the flat land has been sold. When the earthquake hit, their homes fell into the ravines

After the earthquake there was soon a black market in corrugated metal sheeting – the country's main building material

night. But most Guatemalans – almost half of whom are descendants of the proud Mayan Indians, still scratch out an average income of just over one hundred dollars a year by cultivating maize and black beans on lots smaller than the lawns of many suburban homes. And they are still recovering from the horrendous 1973 earthquake.

To them General Romeo Lucas Garcia is only the most recent of a long line of generals – men who in the past have been responsible for a campaign of terror and bloodshed unrestrained since the CIA overthrew Colonel Jacobo Arbenz, the country's last president to come to power through an honest election, in 1954.

Life on Guatemala's 55,000-acre banana plantation has hardly changed since United Brands sold out to Del Monte in 1972. The only access is by rail on Del Monte's trains carry[ing] workers who earn 2.80 dollars a d[ay] while their children work in the pack[ing] sheds. No one is allowed past the gu[ard] post without a pass, and there is [a] Guatemalan army post inside. T[he] union is affiliated to the Washingt[on] based American Institute for Free La[bour] Development, which has worked clos[ely] with the CIA throughout Latin Ameri[ca]. In the evenings North American ov[er] seers relax by their swimming po[ols] look out from their spacious tropi[cal]

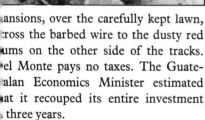

ansions, over the carefully kept lawn,
cross the barbed wire to the dusty red
ums on the other side of the tracks.
el Monte pays no taxes. The Guate-
alan Economics Minister estimated
at it recouped its entire investment
three years.

'Banana trees are like money trees, I
ish I had more of them,' Alfred Eames,
e company chairman, said. It reputedly
ly cost half a million dollars in
acilitation fees' channelled through
el Monte's Panamanian-registered

shipping subsidiaries to a 'local consul-
tant' suggested by the then American
ambassador to obtain Guatemalan ap-
proval for the original sale.

The president then was Carlos
Arana Osorio, who though popular in
business circles has a considerably
different reputation with the peasantry.

Beside the main road in the eastern
province of Zacapa stands a mud-
splashed wooden board. 'Welcome to
Hell', it reads. Behind the barbed wire
fences are the jungle barracks of the

Guatemala City after the earthquake.
The municipal leader who suggested
the homeless should squat on empty
land was machine-gunned to death

Zacapa Panthers: 'Here the best soldiers of the Americas are forged.'
Beginning in 1966 they spearheaded a
wave of terror which left more than
3,000 peasants dead. Arana was in
command. According to *Time* magazine
the American military attaché in Guatemala City provided advice, and the
American Government supplied over

twenty million dollars' worth of supplies. Death squads, the most infamous of which was and still is known as MANO, *Moviemento Anti-communista Nacional Organizado*, took over the killings where the army left off.

When Arana became president in 1970 he declared he had a new mandate 'to pacify the country and end the wave of crime'. He declared a state of siege. In two months 700 people were executed. Over the next three years 15,000 more were murdered or 'disappeared'.

Today the process is repeating itself in areas where American oil companies have asked for exploration rights and along the route where a new highway 'the road of peasant liberation' is being built. Land prices have soared. And peasants reluctant to abandon lands they have traditionally farmed are being forced out.

As the 1976 conference of Guatemalan bishops delicately put it: 'Perhaps the expectation of discovering oil in these regions has awakened immoderate ambitions and has sparked off an unjustified violence that we cannot refrain from denouncing.' Elsewhere, throughout much of the country, labour gangers turn up in villages to recruit Indians to work on large cash crop farms at harvest time. The same men sell the Indians food and alcohol on credit, keeping them perennially in debt. Several of the large land-owners have established gambling dens and bars on the peripheries of their estates to the same effect.

Many of these Indians are more fortunate, however, than the landless poor who made up the overwhelming majority of the 22,000 people killed and 74,000 injured in the earthquake of 4 February 1976. Living in precarious hillside slums on the fringes of Guatemala City, those who survived watched as their homes literally cascaded down ravines. Two weeks after the disaster, when a leading municipal figure suggested the homeless squat on un-

damaged estates, he was promptly machine-gunned to death.

It is hardly surprising that two years ago the citizens of the neighbouring British colony of Belize should have choked on their Kellogg's Corn Flakes when they discovered in each box a little plastic jigsaw map of Central America showing their colony as part of greater Guatemala. Though the Kellogg's spokesman apologized, people in Guatemala have no choice.

The previous President, General Kjell (known popularly as Shell) Laugerud, a Norwegian by background, was elected in 1974 only after the government radio announced amazing gains, against the trend, on his behalf. Many of the opposition leaders were murdered in the months surrounding the polling date. Kjell gave businesses a near free hand. In 1976, for example,

two employees in a strike at Coca-Cola's bottling plant were assassinated while two others narrowly escaped a machine-gun attack outside the factory. The company denied it ever took place. Kjell spoke at the opening of the country's new American- and Canadian-owned 221-million-dollar nickel mine. 'Respect Guatemalan laws and treat our workers well,' he told the firm, EXMIBAL. Then he cautioned the workers to 'treat EXMIBAL well by working hard to earn your salaries'. To observers there he was describing a fairyland of industrial relations in a country drenched in blood.

Under the rule of the new president, Romeo Lucas Garcia, who came into office in March 1978 following a typically confused and suspect election, nothing appears to have changed.

Indians make beautiful handicrafts. But most work as peons on plantations, always in debt to men who sell them alcohol

HAITI

Jean-Claude Duvalier – 'Baby Doc' – is supposedly trying to rid Haiti of the legacy of his infamous father. He has a long way to go. Since 1957 when Papa Doc 'won' the presidential election the country has been the Duvalier family seat and is still the poorest in the Western hemisphere. The United States Agency for International Development calculated in 1976 that ninety per cent of the 5.5 million population had a per capita income of forty US dollars a years earning enough for a one-night birth; few people expect to live beyond forty.

The average worker will spend two years earning enough for a one-night stay in the Habitation Leclerc hotel, opened in 1973 with the promise that it will be 'the most extraordinary, lascivious and decadent place on earth'. The city slums and the shacks on the barren salt flats contrast sharply with the cool mountain homes for the elite, where thousands of gallons are poured into swimming pools while, down below, children have to walk miles with huge buckets to collect water to drink. 'Note modern and primitive life side by side' says the tourist brochure.

Papa Doc, his country immortalized in Graham Greene's *The Comedians*, died in 1971, after a reign of terror, corruption and murder which gave his family an estimated 200 million US dollars tucked away in banks abroad. He had become a megalomaniac, comparing himself to Mao Tse-tung, Lenin and Attaturk. His more celebrated exploits included public advertisements of his butchery. One opponent was shot and then propped up in his favourite armchair on one of Port-au-Prince's main roundabouts. Another was tracked down by his forces to a distant province. Papa Doc had the body decapitated, the head preserved on ice and brought on a tray to his office, where he spent several days alternately staring at it and haranguing it.

Where the bright lighthouse of the nation shines – Presidential Palace

71

The Tontons Macoute, the thousands of shaded gunmen who executed his will and his enemies, have been largely tamed and replaced by the Leopards, a United States trained and equipped commando unit. The influence of the voodooism he used against his superstitious population has lessened. A year after his demise many of his subjects were not sure that *Le Grand Disparu* was not still around. The secret police chief did not help by saying on television: 'Like Christ he has conquered death itself.'

Papa Doc left behind a well-oiled propaganda machine for the bemused nineteen-year-old who inherited the presidency for life. It was soon at work, describing him as 'the bright lighthouse of the nation . . . of divine origin . . . a Messiah . . . the zealous and transcendent architect of the nation.'

He is in fact a swarthy, fleshy man with heavy sideboards and a taste for fast cars, model aeroplanes (his security advisers will not allow him to fly real ones), and karate, which has now become the national sport.

Duvalier has also been making tentative moves towards some sort of liberalization. An amnesty sprung some of the political prisoners from Port-au-Prince gaol, now with a bright illuminated sign like a shop front. Through the authoritative exile newspaper *Haiti-Observateur* they told of hundreds of deaths through tuberculosis, malaria, typhoid and simply going insane. One ex-prisoner watched one of his fellows being eaten by worms as he died, and was forced to lick blood spilt by torturers off the floors.

In 1976 Amnesty International denounced Haiti's prisons as 'amongst the most inhumane in the world'.

Any moves towards liberalization have been constantly thwarted by the 'Duvalierists', known as 'the dinosaurs', and headed by the formidable figure of his mother. This group zoomed to power and wealth along with Papa Doc and are determined not to give it up.

Advanced agriculture in Haiti

'Mama Simone' officially serves as 'the shrewd and loyal adviser to the young leader' and holds a strong influence over him. He has not yet married.

Contradictions abound. The government spends as much time policing the wretched peasantry as helping them, and aid workers are in despair. There are not enough trained personnel to carry out a development programme even if the government wanted to, and help sometimes only strengthens the régime. A typical example was in spring 1977, when drought led to severe electricity rationing because of the shortage of hydro-electric power. Rumblings started about a coup, but the United States sent in diesel generators, power was restored, and the plans subsided.

'Baby Doc' the bright lighthouse of the nation, suitably armed, out with his mother 'Mama Simone' *Gamma*

Duvalier is anxious to attract as many American tourists as he can. The attractions are the divorce mills (one day in court, one day sightseeing), and prostitution using the light-skinned 'horizontales' imported in their hundreds from the neighbouring Dominican Republic. The main barrier to Haiti becoming the brothel of Eastern America is the VD rate, reckoned to be amongst the highest in the world.

Americans have moved in for other reasons as well. Dozens of light industries exploit the rock-bottom wages, plentiful labour, and (until recently) guaranteed lack of strikes. Haiti is now the world's largest manufacturer of baseballs.

Duvalier has to be cautious in case his country becomes a target for Carter's human rights programme. In May 1977 he sacked a senior minister (suspected of having personally supervised the massacre of 100 people thirteen years previously), after *Haiti-Observateur* published a secret World Bank report which revealed that more than half the ninety-five-million-dollar public revenue in 1975 was 'credited directly to 300 or so special accounts . . . for a multitude of unspecified purposes'. And his tentative moves, backed by the US, have often been stopped in their tracks by the ensuing trouble. In December 1977 two new weekly papers aimed at young people started reporting an unprecedented series of strikes and demonstrations by workers demanding more pay. The Duvalierists put the pressure on, a committee of three ministers was set up to carry out a press clampdown, and both papers were closed.

At the same time the French, who lost control in 1804 when the slaves threw them out, and the Americans have been vying for Haiti's economic advantages and strategic importance fifty miles north of Cuba. The US has a large naval base on the south coast.

Whilst 'Le Gros Michelin' lazes in his palace, surrounded by machine-guns mounted in bunkers on the low walls, and ancient anti-aircraft guns poking up in the flower-beds, the aid battle has degenerated to garbage collection, where the Americans seem to have won with a fleet of monster red dustbin lorries. The French interest was explained by one of their cabinet ministers as 'the expansion of culture throughout the Americas in accordance with France's spiritual mission'. They are helped by the fact that only the top ten per cent of Haitian society speaks French. The rest do not understand it. They speak Creole, a French-based language of the former slaves, and cannot read, understand or afford' the glossy French magazines bought by the elite.

There are doubts about how long Duvalier will last. Kennedy cut off aid to his father in disgust and Nixon and Kissinger brought him back into the fold (the US ambassador said on television that Haiti was 'a free country'). They have now gone and in 1977 the 400,000 Haitians living in exile were finally granted asylum. Previously they had been classified as 'economic refugees' and sixty per cent were therefore categorized as illegal immigrants.

On 22 September 1977, the twentieth anniversary of the Duvalier family dynasty, Allard K. Lowenstein, the United States Deputy Ambassador at the UN, took the unprecedented step of publicly joining the exiles on the platform at a meeting in Manhattan called to denounce the tyranny.

Slum conditions in Haiti

HONDURAS

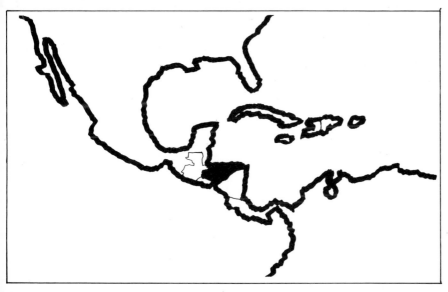

Honduras is the original banana republic. It used to be run by a man who started life as a bus station time-keeper. According to the publicity material sent to the authors by the London embassy in February 1978, he is still running it as 'the constitutional President' heading a national congress, democratically elected.

The publicity material refers to the government in 1965. Since then the time-keeper has gone, come back, and gone again. The present ruler is Colonel Juan Alberto Melgar Castro (no relation), who used to be the chief of police.

He has decided to run the country with a twelve-man cabinet of ten civilian technocrats and two military men. The young lieutenant-colonels who put him in power keep an eye on things behind the scenes.

On past form Melgar should have been overthrown by now. Honduras has had more than 120 presidential changes since it declared its independence from Spain in 1821. Most have involved the military. None have done much good for the three million population. Their country is the second least developed and poorest in the Western hemisphere. Haiti, the family seat of the Duvaliers, is the first.

Most are a mix of the original Indians and the Spanish settlers who ruthlessly exploited them in the silver mines. The Spaniards won control of the country in the 1530s by killing the Indian chief Lempira at a peace parley. His name is now immortalized as the country's virtually worthless monetary unit.

The majority scratch a living on the pieces of land which are not covered by dense forests, stands of pine regularly devastated by fire and bark beetle, or vast banana plantations.

The average farmer produces little more in a year than a normal Western family eats in a week. Thousands of peasants have to live in grass-roofed mud huts, existing on a staple diet of tasteless tortillas. According to medical experts half a million Honduran chil-

Banana float. Politics begin here

retired to become simple commander-in-chief of the army. Two years previously, in the same role, he had led his forces into battle against next-door El Salvador in the brief and bloody 'Football War' triggered off by a referee's decision at a match. He lost.

In 1973 he decided to make a comeback and overthrew Dr Ramon Cruz, the shy retiring lawyer who had been constitutional head of state and was finding the nitty-gritty of Honduran politics too alarming for him. Cruz retired gracefully.

Lopez's government was totally incapable of dealing with the devastation of Fifi. The entire country was a disaster area. Grain intended as aid relief was eaten by rats on Caribbean port docksides hundreds of miles away because no transport was arranged. When it arrived the dense forests and the destruction of the communications network made distribution to some of the hardest-hit areas virtually impossible.

Lopez was trying to fend off the mounting criticism when he was finished off by the banana bribe scandal, along with the chairman of United Brands, Mr Eli Black.

United Brands Inc., an American multi-national with 200,000 acres of plantations, had previously been the centre of much controversy for its role in Honduran politics. In February 1975 Mr Eli Black showed how far it was involved. He got up from his desk on the forty-fourth floor of the Pan-Am building in central Manhattan, New York, smashed the window with his executive briefcase, and jumped 800 feet to his death.

The US Securities and Exchange Commission investigated and uncovered a bribe of 1.25 million dollars paid into a Swiss bank account, in return for which the Honduras military régime had reduced its tax on each box of bananas from one dollar to twenty-five cents. The annual saving to United Brands was estimated at 7.5 million dollars.

A parallel inquiry in Honduras named

dren are suffering from malnutrition which will either kill them or give them irreparable brain, eye, or ear damage.

Their misery is compounded by natural disasters like Hurricane Fifi, which hit the country on 18 September 1974 with wind-gusts of up to one hundred miles per hour and over thirty inches of rain in twenty-four hours. Whole mountain sides fell away, carrying with them 5,000 dead and making 500,000 homeless. The handling of the ensuing chaos was one of the reasons for the downfall of the time-keeper, General Lopez Arellano, the supposed strongman of the country.

Lopez, after handing the country over to a civilian president in 1971, had

the recipient as the former Finance Minister, Abraham Bennaton, now known as 'Bananaton'. The commission head, Jorge Arturo Reina, said it had been unable to determine whether any of the money had been passed on to the (now deposed) Lopez.

Melgar's government is now working for its proclaimed ends of national unity and social justice, and what one member described as 'better distribution of what little wealth we have'.

United Brands is still exporting half a ton of bananas per head of the population from the country.

Working towards better distribution of what wealth we have. Slum conditions in Honduras

INDONESIA

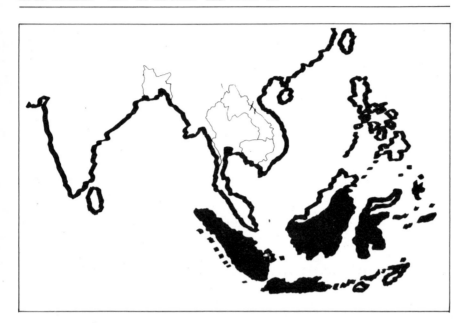

'Growing within the fertile Indonesian archipelago is another archipelago – an archipelago of prisons and penal colonies . . . Indonesia is a tropical Gulag.'

Amnesty International

To be released from Indonesia's penal colonies, political internees have to answer over four hundred questions, part of a psychological test. 'Which do you prefer, kissing women or eating in a restaurant?' 'Do you like to read newspapers that report about crime or about mountain expeditions?' are typical. The prisoners, of course, have seen neither women, restaurants nor mountains since being incarcerated in 1965 following an American-supported military take-over led by General Suharto after which an estimated half million communists, trade unionists and local politicians were murdered. 'What will you do if you find you don't agree with the government's policy?' is a question closer to home.

'We cannot read people's thoughts,' explained Admiral Sudomo, head of the

Suharto and his wife, Tien (Tien-percent). Her business empire stretches across South-East Asia

Job applicants for work with multi-national companies in Indonesia must have good conduct certificates from the police

Indonesian political prisoners have to grow their own food – or starve. Now they are being shipped to new settlements, financed by the World Bank

secret police, Chief of Staff of KOPKAMTIB, Command for the Restoration of Security and Order, in December last year. 'By means of psycho-tests, we can measure their knowledge of ideological matters and then check this with the report of their interrogation. Observations are taken every six months. It is estimated that the results are sixty to seventy per cent accurate.'

At least one-third of the prisoners, and there are anywhere between 20,000 and 90,000 of them, depending on which estimates one accepts, are being re-classified as die-hards and will remain in gaol. They call themselves 'tapols' meaning political prisoners, though the term has been banned. In effect they are what remains of the first post-Dutch colonial generation of educated Indonesians who were not either businessmen or soldiers.

These latter run the country now, with economists trained in American universities on Ford Foundation and other grants. The results have been dramatic. In 1975 Pertamina, the national oil company, became the only OPEC state oil company to go bankrupt, with ten billion dollars' worth of debts. The general who ran it, Ibnu Sutowo, though he officially drew a salary of 300 dollars a month, has several houses and a Rolls-Royce. He obviously has had other sources of income. His wife's Mercedes Benzes are white, his daughter's are brown, and his son's are green. The company has been co-financing property speculation, building luxury hotels and suburban bungalows, financing private airways, insurance companies and private commodity deals – in all of which high ranking military men were involved. Suharto's wife, Tien (known as Tien-per-cent), keeps a string of private trading companies and hotels throughout South-East Asia. The much heralded 'green revolution', which was to transform Indonesian agriculture, became so corrupt in dealing with agri-business corporations that Suharto

This man, a *tapol*, though in a remote island concentration camp, is regularly interrogated to find out what he thinks

Suharto sometimes dares to visit the countryside, to show he is still alive and in power

had to insist the whole affair be handled out of court.

On the other hand, Indonesians on average are shorter under Suharto's 'New Order' than they were before, due to malnutrition. Last year, famine was reported less than an hour's drive from the capital, Jakarta. According to a recent survey people are worse off than they were in 1968.

Devout Muslims bewail the 'drift towards corruption and moral decay'. But a succession of anti-corruption campaigns has had little effect. The generals still go to the same nightclubs and massage parlours, and expect their bribes. They can because Indonesia is so bountiful in natural resources – oil, timber, rubber and natural gas – that foreign governments and banks willingly guarantee their overdraft and stabilize the currency, quite aside from conditions for the country's 140 million inhabitants. The Intergovernmental Group on Indo-

nesia, made up of the World Bank, the International Monetary Fund, the Asian Development Bank, Japan and most Western governments, loans the country more than two billion dollars a year. Russia's new fourteen-storey embassy on Jakarta's main street dwarfs other diplomatic compounds. British Royal Navy ships cruise into Jakarta harbour literally packed to the gunwales with weaponry for sale from over sixty British firms. The Germans are selling Indonesia submarines, the Australians provide reconnaissance aircraft, and France sells tanks. This is dwarfed by United States military aid, which under the Carter administration increased to a record fifty-eight million dollars for 1978.

In 1975 Indonesia invaded what was formerly Portuguese East Timor, using American C-130 Hercules transport planes, armed, according to the US State Department, ninety per cent with

American weapons. It is estimated that 100,000 East Timorese have been killed. In the South Molucca Islands, members of the national autonomy movement are being rounded up and gaoled.

The first *topols* to be released late last year came from the concentration camp on the crocodile-infested jungle island of Buru, two thousand miles, a plane ride and three boat trips from Jakarta. They were mostly old men suffering from tuberculosis. Many were crippled. Some had to be carried on stretchers. Dutifully they read an oath of allegiance to President Suharto, swore not to sue the government, agreed that all actions taken against them were necessary, and denounced Marxism. None of them had ever had a trial. A few went home to their families. But most are being moved on to 'transmigration settlements' being built on Indonesia's less densely settled islands. These are part of a World Bank-financed popula-

tion control scheme. And unless 200,000 people are 'settled' by this year, the government will not qualify for the first part of a massive World Bank loan.

Travelling in the opposite direction are orang-utans captured in the jungles chopped down for homes in Japan, and brought to Jakarta where they are kept as pets.

In January this year students throughout the country called for 'clean government'. The universities were closed, the leaders arrested. And Jakarta's leading newspapers were shut. The editors had until 10 A.M. on 1 February to sign statements written on notepaper bearing the newspaper's letterheading pledging to remember that their papers were 'co-responsible' for maintaining national stability, would put state interests above all else, respect government press regulations, and willingly engage in 'introspection and correction'.

The next morning Admiral Sudomo, letters in hand, apologized to the editors for the inconvenience while serving them coffee in his office. Then he asked them two more small favours – not to report student political activities or publish statements from the régime's most prominent critics before the People's Congress (MPR) selected a new President at the end of March. Needless to say, Suharto was chosen again. And Sudomo was promoted.

Indonesia's Green Revolution. Now collapsed because of bribes and mismanagement

Food hoarding in Jakarta has led to massive wastage due to rats

IRAN

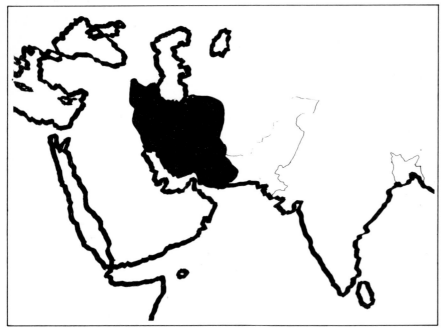

Mohammad Reza Pahlavi, the fifty-nine-year-old Shah of Iran, who crowned himself and his wife, Farah, in 1967, is the son of a Cossack colonel, the grandson of a peasant. Since 1941 he has reigned over the mountains and deserts of what was once Persia, a bulwark against the Soviet Union, and a near inexhaustible supply of oil for Britain and the United States.

Without these allies he would never have survived. When his father abdicated on his behalf the peasants rose in revolt against the royal estates, beating officials and burning houses built on lands confiscated and extorted by him. The income from those estates is now channelled through the Shah's private Pahlavi Foundation, complete with Geneva bank account, out of which leading Western and Iranian public personalities have been paid millions of pounds.

In 1953 he fled to Rome, where he conferred with Allen Dulles, head of the CIA, while one of his generals and the CIA agent Kermit Roosevelt staged a coup, arresting the Prime Minister, Mohammad Mosaddeq, whose first act had been to nationalize Iran's oil. Dollars became the official currency in Tehran on the day. Bus and taxi drivers shuttling gangs armed with knives and clubs and shouting 'Down with Mosaddeq' proudly waved wads of bills in their hands.

As Anthony Eden, then British Foreign Minister, wrote: 'The news of Mosaddeq's fall from power reached me during my convalescence when my wife and I, with my son, were cruising the Mediterranean between Greek islands. I slept happily that night.'

The last but one American ambassador to Iran was Richard Helms, previously head of the CIA, who played an active role in the Watergate affair. The current ambassador is a man named Sullivan, known for his involvement in the saturation bombing of Laos during the Vietnam War, and ambassador to the Philippines when President Marcos suspended the constitution and declared a state of siege there.

The United States trained and armed the Shah's police. British ex-commandos act as guards at the exclusive gambling casino surrounded by barbed wire and used by members of the royal family near the Caspian Sea. The Shah is commander-in-chief of the armed forces and appoints the head of SAVAK, the secret police set up in 1957 to root out 'any kind of conspiracy detrimental to public interests'. Over 60,000 agents are paid to lurk in villages listening to whispering women, tap telephones, follow visitors' taxis, sit in on any meetings overseas at which Iranian students participate. They make arrests at their own discretion, and hold 'suspects' incommunicado until just before appearing before military tribunals which pass sentence under a penal code that provides the death penalty for the merest dissent. Opposition among the thirty-five million Iranians is intolerable to the Shah. The country has one party, the National Political Resurrection Movement, which he established in 1975, saying that anyone who refused to join could either go into exile or to prison.

Iranians travelling overseas are afraid to speak frankly for fear their relatives at home will disappear. Though the exact number is not known, tens of thousands of political prisoners are in gaol, despite batches let out to commemorate anniversaries and new years. The Shah always denies they are tortured. But when journalists managed to contact some late last year, they were given sworn statements describing barbarous mutilations ranging from electric shock, beatings, burning and raping a suspect's daughter in front of him to pushing hot irons through prisoners' cheeks and shooting them 'while trying to escape'.

Yet the Shah's 'White Revolution', his 'Shah-people revolution' for building a 'great civilization' by the end of the century out of the country's oil revenues

The Shah

which amount to an estimated twenty-three billion dollars this year, has been taking a buffeting of late.

Jimmy Carter flew to Tehran last autumn pointedly to impress upon him that Iran's strategic interests, as grandiose as they may be, do not extend as far as aiding Somalia in the Ethiopian war. Pahlavi would have to remain content with having annexed half a dozen islands in the Arabian Gulf, and having sent troops to fight against mountain-based guerillas in Oman, where, according to British officers who advised them, they performed miserably. Carter also guaranteed more arms shipments to add to his massive military stockpile. How to keep it from rusting, falling into disrepair or simply becoming obsolete, has been one of the Shah's major preoccupations. Quite aside from his noted soft spot for buying virtually any new piece of military design which arms salesmen impress upon him, the Shah now has the biggest tank force in the Middle East after Israel, over 160 F-16 jet fighters which are so sophisticated that only the best American pilots fly them, a complete border radar and missile system, a whole city building Bell helicopters, a tank factory and armaments repair yard, seven flying radar stations capable of carrying out internal surveillance, and much else. He has bought more than eighteen billion dollars' worth of military supplies from the United States alone in the last five years, the fastest and most unproductive way possible to spend the country's newly acquired oil revenues. Richard Nixon secretly agreed he could have any piece of American hardware he wanted, short of nuclear weapons. So there are now over 30,000 Americans in Iran working in maintenance shops and airfields. The Senate Foreign Relations Committee concluded last year that: 'it is unlikely that Iran could go to war in the next five to ten years with its current inventory without US support on a day-to-day basis'.

Washington police kept protesting Iranian students away from the Shah
with tear gas last year, but it drifted back in Jimmy Carter's eyes *Gamma*

The Shah handing over some land
deeds to keep the peasants happy

If the Shah is looking for enemies he has plenty at home, and now they are beginning to speak out. Not only the various regional groups and workers; also lawyers, academics, and Muslim leaders are demanding a return to some sort of parliamentary rule, civil liberties, a free press, and open debate.

On 8 February thousands of demonstrators ran riot through the streets of the beautiful city of Tabriz, wrecking banks, cinemas and government buildings. They were shouting 'Death to the Shah!' It was the first serious demonstration against him since 1963. The Shah was upset, calling them 'red-black reactionaries', 'foreign agitators'.

'Work, work, and more work' is the only slogan he wants followed, as he explained in a recent book.

He sacked the chief of the Tabriz secret police. And the demonstration was put down in the traditional way – with British- and American-made tanks and machine-guns, instead of tear gas or water hoses. But the bazaars were closed in protest, and Muslim leaders denounced the Shah, saying the government provoked the riot. The Tabriz demonstration had been held, in fact, to commemorate forty days of mourning for the people shot down by trigger-happy security forces in the religious city of Qom.

But Iranians want more than just basic human rights. The Shah has encouraged multi-national corporations to cultivate pistachio nuts, strawberries and asparagus to be sold in Europe and the United States on lands which once belonged to peasants who now turn their goats loose at night to eat the crops. He has squandered hundreds of millions of dollars on extravagant schemes such

The Shah. Is he still America's puppet? He prefers not to talk about SAVAK, his secret police

as contracting for massive hospitals, sold him by a British lord on behalf of a British consortium, complete with nurses and bedside lamps, only to find he was being grossly overcharged. Three years ago he decided to launch an anti-corruption campaign with mobile courts manned by students, but only after his wife, Farah, noticed a mere admiral's wife wearing a jewelled brooch which she herself had turned down as too expensive when presented to her shortly before by a merchant from Switzerland.

British police advisers, quite prepared to work elsewhere in the Middle East, refuse to go to Iran. They describe the Shah's prisons as 'toe-nail factories', saying all that comes out is toe-nails and screams.

KAMPUCHEA

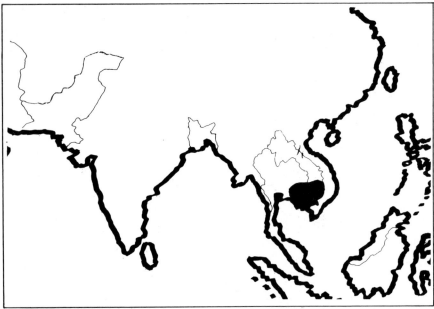

Democratic Kampuchea (Cambodia) is the world's leading example of 'socialist nepotism'. The Prime Minister, Pol Pot, alias Soloth Sar, head of the Kampuchean Communist Party is married to the sister of the Minister of Social Action, Ieng Thirith. She is the wife of the Foreign Minister, Ieng Sary, while the Minister of Youth and Culture, Mrs Yun Yat, is the wife of the Minister of Defence, Son Sen. The three couples, or 'Gang of Six' as they are called, have had a heavy hand in Cambodian Communist – Khmer Rouge – affairs.

Democratic Kampuchea is also drenched in blood. So much so that it has been written into the national anthem. According to Pol Pot, 'Its essence is the blood of our entire people, of those who fell for centuries past . . . This blood has been turned into class and national indignation.'

The sentiment is well appreciated in Kampuchea where Khmer peasants have traditionally been moved to cut out their enemy's liver, usually as vengeance against the neighbouring Thais and Vietnamese who have ravaged their

tiny country for centuries. The United States, for its part, dropped over 539,000 tons of bombs on Cambodian rice-paddies and forests. South Vietnamese pilots even paid bribes for the privilege of bombing defenceless Cambodia every day of the week. South Vietnamese troops indiscriminately terrorized the Khmer countryside, seizing livestock and forcing peasants to buy them back.

According to many historians the Khmer peasants see the capital, Phnom-Penh, as the creation of French colonialists and Chinese businessmen. So when the Americans fled Phnom-Penh in their helicopters on 12 April 1975, leaving 2.5 million mostly desperate and confused people with only enough rice for eight days, the country's holocaust seemed bound to enter yet another stage.

Collaborators, reportedly, were shot on sight. Thousands tried to flee to Thailand and Vietnam but were caught and shot. Many lost their way in the jungles, caught dysentery and died. The rest of the population was force-marched back to the countryside. The

lucky ones were taken in by villagers to live in garrison-like cooperative farms. Others were rounded up and driven across the country as forced labour squads. Many died by the roadsides, unused to physical effort and emotional strain. Summary justice was meted out by war-hardened adolescents who carry guns.

It has been a civil war that the government's closest allies, the North Koreans, never knew, compounded by malaria and starvation.

Western anti-communists claim that as many as 1.2 million people died. They even cite as proof interviews which have been shown to be bogus. A truer figure would seem to be at least several hundred thousand. It is hardly surprising that Pol Pot should have closed the borders.

Much of Phnom-Penh is now said to be covered with weeds. Prince Sihanouk, who fought with the Communist Khmer Rouge against the Americans after the CIA deposed him in 1970, has been tending his garden, or writing his memoirs, depending on which account one believes. A small diplomatic community, confined to its embassies, has had little to do but read the official daily bulletin and attend occasional receptions.

But the Indochina war goes on. Vietnam and Kampuchea almost daily have accused each other of unspeakable atrocities. Since December last year several divisions of Vietnam troops have dug in deep inside Kampuchea, while Pol Pot has several times announced that 'traitors have been eradicated', referring to Khmers trained in and loyal to Hanoi.

The 'Gang of Six' has settled with General Kriangsak in Thailand over skirmishes which both sides provoked. Inside Kampuchea the government, supported by China and North Korea, and bristling with Maoist rhetoric, remains undeterred from its chosen path of national reconstruction. Rice production has increased. Fields devastated by

Pol Pot. The brains of the Kampuchean revolution. The cities are empty. Everyone works in the fields. And the Vietnamese have already invaded
Camera Press

American bombs are now producing two crops a year.

But in achieving their more profound objective – ensuring the survival of the Khmers as a people, who now number about seven million, a little less than the population of Paris – the régime may be failing. Overcrowding, prolonged emotional stress combined with much of the trained medical class having been wiped out has meant that women are having miscarriages and their periods ceasing.

Whether children can be born and raised in current circumstances remains to be seen. Yet among the lucky to be living there are few who now dare question what is officially referred to synonymously as 'revolutionary justice' and the Cambodian national dream.

KOREA

Korea is probably the most ethnically homogeneous country in the world, virtually without national minorities; and is governed by two régimes – competing, disseminating false propaganda, and regularly threatening to usurp one another's right to speak for all Koreans. At the end of the Korean war in 1953 there were said to be only two buildings left standing in the capital of the North, Pyongyang. The Americans had bombed towns, bridges and the irrigation system so heavily that Air Force generals complained there were no targets left. They also used napalm for the first time. The capital of the South, Seoul, was flooded with refugees, American GIs and intelligence agents.

Today 42,000 American troops are still there. The South Korean military has been entirely equipped by the United States, except for uniforms and food. And though Jimmy Carter has said most American troops would be withdrawn, the arsenal of American tactical nuclear weapons deployed there will stay.

North Korea is run by the Korean Workers' Party led by the 'fatherly, beloved' and much idolized Kim Il Sung. Few non-socialist state visitors are allowed in, except for Japanese businessmen. Virtually no information is available regarding whether there is capital punishment, or if political dissidents are locked up.

South Korea is run by President Chung Hee Park, in collaboration with the army and the Korean CIA, closely counselled by their American and Japanese counterparts. Torture, political assassinations, political imprisonment and arbitrary arrest are widespread.

Both parts of the country are scenically beautiful. North Korea has fifteen million people. The South has thirty-five millions. Both, in their popular culture, idolize modern consumerism – a television in every home, men dressed in Western-style clothes, women in more traditional Korean fashion.

Both place priority on economic

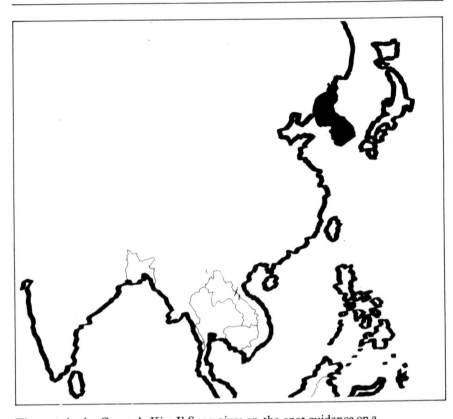

The great leader Comrade Kim Il Sung gives on-the-spot guidance on a construction site to put into practice his grand plan for the construction of Pyongyang

growth and military defence. But in the North people spend only two to three per cent of their incomes on housing. Rice costs about 0.15 dollars per pound, the same price as a cinema ticket. Televisions cost about fifty dollars. All children go to school for ten years. Medicine also is free. Men and women earn the same. And there are no taxes. According to visitors, Pyongyang is cleaner, more spacious and people live better than in Peking. It is also the most disciplined, uniform society in the world. Everything is always perfect, they say. On the other hand, Seoul is a typical Third World capital, with five and a half million people – a wealthy metropolis surrounded by belching factories and sprawling slums lacking rudimentary sanitation. The infant mortality rate is thirty-eight per thousand. One out of every thirty people has tuberculosis. Rice costs half the average family's income. But there too almost everyone is literate. And the South's Gross National Product per capita is higher than in the North, 700 dollars compared to 200 dollars.

Kim Il Sung wants to reunify the country. Park needs desperately for the Americans to stay on.

Kim Il Sung Square in the heart of Pyongyang

The Democratic People's Republic of Korea (North)

Everyone is always happy in North Korea

Pyongyang after American bombing during the Korean War

Outside Kim Il Sung university, as under the seventy-foot-high bronze statue of Kim Il Sung, inside the Kim Il Sung museum, in Kim Il Sung Square in Pyongyang, as under pictures of Kim Il Sung in every home, factory and shop, Kim Il Sung's 'Juche' idea guides the peace-loving socialist people of North Korea in their every thought and task. Picture books show children 'dressed in winter clothes provided by fatherly Marshal Kim Il Sung'. They show 'the great leader Comrade Kim Il Sung answering the enthusiastic cheers of the construction workers'. Kim Il Sung: 'The ever-victorious iron-willed brilliant commander and the outstanding military strategist, and his Juche-based strategy and tactics and immortal feats

92

performed in defeating US imperialism and defending the freedom and independence of the fatherland!'

So who is he? He is sixty-five and he has a lump on his neck which Romanian doctors probe from time to time and which South Koreans speculate is malignant. The Kim Il Sung museum in Pyongyang, the capital, slips from hard, incontestable photographs into 'artists' reconstructions' in portraying the great leader's revolutionary career up until he returned from Moscow to Korea under the Soviet occupation of the North at the end of the Second World War. Photographs show him then dressed in a very snappy white suit, striped tie and Panama hat – hardly what one would wear on a 'Long March' as in China. The photographs disappear again for the Korean war period.

School children do not have to visit the museum, though they all do, to learn about their great leader. He has, reportedly, visited almost every village in the North. But strangely there are no photographs of these tours either. Nonetheless, with Mao for so long a neighbour, and Stalin so long a mentor, North Koreans have taken their own personality cult very seriously.

The year 1976 was the high point of hagiographic fervour. Foreign policy was simplified to placing full-page excerpts of 'Kim Il Sung thought' throughout the Western press. North Korean comrade diplomats smuggled dope, tobacco and liquor partly to pay for them, until they were caught in Scandinavia.

And the illustrious leader's own son, Kim Chong Il, now thirty-seven years old, was widely touted as the Republic's next leader. Kim Junior's promotion has been meteoric. In 1967, after he had been to pilot-training school in East Germany, he was appointed responsible for no less than reissuing party membership cards after a purge of 'counter-revolutionary and anti-party elements'. (The party now has two million members.) In 1970 he became

The great leader Comrade Kim Il Sung among children

party deputy director of both organization and guidance and culture and arts. In 1973 he was promoted to party secretary, again in charge of organization, propaganda and agitation. And the next year he reportedly was in charge of relations with South Korea and Japan. Then the problems started. Though the North produces a remarkable eight million tons of rice a year, the oil price rise pushed up foreign expenditure, while the world price of non-ferrous metals, the North's main exports, fell. The government was forced to reschedule its 1.5 billion dollars' worth of foreign loans, much of it with Japan, built up over the previous

three years buying heavy equipment and whole factories, such as complete cement works, to make economic big leaps forward, called 'challima'.

Both the Soviet Union and China immediately cut back their lending, from over 750 million dollars during the previous five years, to less than six million dollars combined for 1977.

The North Koreans appointed an economist with industrial experience, Mr Li Jong-Ok, as Premier, and began asking themselves if Kim Jr, as impeccable as his pedigree might be, was really

One of the main streets, Pyongyang

the best comrade to be president during these difficult times.

At the beginning of this year rumours circulated that he had narrowly escaped an assassination attempt. That a struggle has been going on within the party is undeniable. But whether Kim Sr bought 40,000 gold Swiss watches bearing portraits of himself and his son to give to loyal party cadres on his sixty-fifth birthday, 15 April, as has been reported, has to be seen to be believed. Though fatherly Kim's health is failing, the people will not forget his 'Juche' idea. 'In a nutshell,' Kim Il Sung wrote, 'the idea of Juche means that the masters of the revolution and construction are the masses of the people. In other words, it is an idea that one is responsible for one's own destiny and that one has also the capacity of hewing out one's own destiny.' Salutary as this may seem, visitors to North Korea say they are not sure what it has to do with the ordinary people walking along the road who automatically salute as large saloon cars carrying party officials speed by, often knocking the people over.

Republic of Korea (South)

Major-General, now President for life, Chung Hee Park, an ex-officer in the Japanese Imperial Army, has decreed that South Korea will be ruled by the 'Yushin' (revitalizing) constitution which he approved, and nothing else.

Kim Dae Jung, fifty-three, his opponent in the 1971 election which Park won following widespread electoral fraud, is now in solitary confinement in Seoul's West Gate prison, refusing to sign a statement admitting any guilt or asking for pardon. Kim was kidnapped from a Tokyo hotel in 1973, and only saved from being dropped into the sea with stones tied to his wrists at the last minute.

In August 1976 Kim and seventeen other venerable and aged opposition figures – most of them leading clergymen of South Korea's four million Christians – and a former president, were sentenced to from two to five years in gaol for reading out a statement in a church calling for a return to constitutional rule.

Children are glad to wear winter clothes provided by the fatherly Marshal Kim Il Sung

Seoul. Money and squalor mixed. Japanese businessmen and American GIs come for the strip clubs and bar girls

President Ford demonstrating for the press the friendly, close relations between the United States and its ally, President Park *Camera Press*

It has been seventeen years since Chung Hee Park took over by coup, and six years since he declared martial law, suspended the constitution and introduced the first of his anti-communist and anti-opposition decrees. Political life is controlled by Emergency Measure No. 9, decreed on 13 May 1975. It is a crime punishable by up to fifteen years in prison to advocate any changes in the 'Yushin' constitution, broadcast or publish any criticisms of it, hold critical student demonstrations, abscond overseas with Korean property, and report any criticism of Measure No. 9 itself. The decree, Park explained, is intended to 'consolidate national unity and coalesce national opinion'.

Student protests are ruthlessly and instantly crushed. When Park's wife was assassinated by a bullet intended for him while he was addressing a memorial service in Seoul's national theatre in August 1974, the gunman was immediately branded as an agent of Kim Il Sung, and hanged.

Park is maintained in power by the army, and the Korean CIA which is reputed to have over 20,000 agents and even more informers working on what has been described as the 'classic basis of seduction, pay-off and intimidation'. Park reputedly gets a cut of many of the country's large commercial contracts. And he regularly has Japanese and American congressmen bribed through agents, such as the irrepressible Tong Sun Park who scattered hundreds of thousands of dollars around Washington in what is known as 'Operation White Snow'. The evangelical Reverend Moon also used to set out on fund-raising evangelical tours in Europe and the United States on the government's behalf. With the opposition New Democratic party hopelessly rent by petty squabbling, and business booming, Park apparently has little to worry about.

South Korea has a growth rate of over eight per cent per year. Exports have increased over twenty times since he took power. Over half a million

Korean labourers will be shipped overseas by 1980 to work on construction contracts supervised by the Korean CIA. (A revolt by Korean workers in West Germany a few years ago was quickly hushed up.)

Young Korean women have flooded the massage parlours and nightclubs of Tokyo and Yokohama, Japan. And over 400,000 unaccompanied Japanese men visit South Korea yearly, many of them, as the saying goes, flying over just for 'a night on the town'. By selling his people Park generates foreign exchange. And with wages the lowest in Asia and trade unions banned, foreign investors have been suitably impressed.

The United States government has subsidized the state with over twelve billion dollars in military and economic aid since the end of the Korean war. The Japanese have outdone American investors, though, in pumping more than one billion dollars more than the Americans into capital goods.

Nonetheless, South Korea is caught on an economic treadmill. Unless its exports, which are mainly textiles, electronics and its own people, keep selling abroad, and at an ever increasing rate and price, the country will fall faster behind in paying off interest on its massive (over twelve billion dollars) and still growing foreign debt.

In the past Park's remedy for economic problems has been to lower real wages in his high finance state. At the same time he has simply declared a national emergency or revealed another hair-raising plot, allegedly from Kim Il Sung. Anyone who has challenged him has been locked up.

Investors have not complained. But it has dawned on the American administration, and several banks, that it is worth their while assessing how much longer the Korean people will accept fanatical anti-communism as the official national palliative, and as an adequate explanation of why they are working so hard to remain perpetually in debt.

NICARAGUA

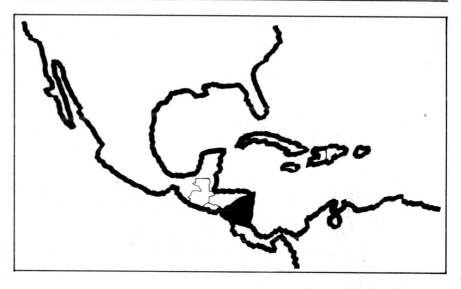

Anastasio Somoza, Nicaragua's potbellied potentate, crony of Richard Nixon and Howard Hughes, who controls everything in Nicaragua's capital, Managua, from trash collection and parking meters to importing Mercedes Benz saloons used exclusively by the police, is supposed to be number one on the American government's list of unacceptable despots.

Yet, strangely, the CIA has not seen fit to overthrow him. Nonetheless every time local guerillas – Sandinistas – slip over the border from Honduras and Costa Rica, to machine-gun one of Anastasio's ('Tachito's') National Guard posts or kidnap a government minister, hopes rise throughout Central America.

Small children with gastroenteritis and other diarrhoea diseases account for one out of five deaths in Nicaragua, which reportedly has the world's highest homicide rate, and the highest rate of alcoholism in Central America. Not mentioned in official statistics are the hundreds of poor farmers and their families who have 'disappeared' following visits from the National Guard in the past few years. Priests have been filing sworn affidavits that armed government patrols have descended on villages, raping women, torturing and butchering the men, smashing and looting their homes. Over two hundred 'campesinos' (farmers) and their families 'disappeared' between 1975 and 1977 in one rural province alone.

Tachito, who is both President and 'Jefe Supremo' of the armed forces, has hired a Washington Public Relations firm, MacKenzie McCheyne Inc., to convince American congressmen this is not so. And with noticeable results. Last summer both the American Senate and House of Representatives voted to continue topping up the over twenty million dollars the US government has spent on military aid to Somoza's security forces over the past years. Nicaraguan National Guardsmen get their training in their 'counter-terror' methods from US advisers at the School of the Americas in the Panama Canal Zone.

According to close relatives the 'Jefe Supremo' is characterized by self-exaltation, megalomania and self-deification. According to a survey of National Guard attitudes carried out in the early seventies, his cadets espoused 'a mono-

American advisers teach Nicaraguan
cadets to parade. Many of them are
more interested in bribes

maniacal concern with national security'.

But this doesn't mean Somoza can rally his troops by appeals to patriotism alone. After the earthquake on 23 December 1972 which reduced Managua to rubble, not one company of National Guards could be formed. The then American Ambassador, Turner Shelton, who reportedly cannot speak Spanish, encouraged Somoza to seize absolute power, suggesting that American troops would be on call. But the situation was soon under control. With over 8,000 people killed by the earthquake, 50,000 homes destroyed and over eighty per cent of commercial property in Managua in ruins, a massive reconstruction programme was required. The National Guard were given first priority in repairs and building new homes. And as if from nowhere a flourishing market in bribes sprang up – for guarding damaged property, issuing building permits, import licences and even distributing relief agency food.

To keep the National Guard promotion system from becoming overloaded now, Somoza retires whole classes of cadets from the Military Academy on full pay. For nearly twenty years he himself had been 'Jefe Director' of the National Guard. When he graduated from West Point in 1946, his father, Anastasio I (or 'Tacho'), who had been put in power by US Marines, gave his son a command. And when Tacho was finally assassinated in 1956, Tachito and his brother Luis (who died in 1967) stepped quickly into his shoes. In 1967 Anastasio II ran for the presidency. During the riots before the election more than forty people were killed and over one hundred wounded. The result was a foregone conclusion. As Somoza said to the dispirited opposition, 'You won the election, but I won the count.'

With an unabashed combination of American patronage and political violence the Somoza family has transformed

Papa Somoza (right), in 1928, learning table manners from US marine officers during Thanksgiving Day dinner. A few years later they put him in power

'Jefe Supremo' having a good laugh

the Nicaraguan economy into a well-nigh impregnable and extremely lucrative fief. With a personal fortune estimated at about 150 million dollars, Tachito and relatives own the national airline, national shipping company, banks, hotels, radio, television and the press, as well as most of the country's small but fast-growing manufacturing sector – all made possible by massive unsecured government loans.

Today in Managua the cathedral still stands, but most of the rest of what was the city is covered in wild flowers and

Papa Somoza, with his sons Anastasio and Luis. The family has run Nicaragua for forty years

weeds, not rebuilt since the earthquake, except for a few buildings on properties owned by Somoza.

Last year there was talk of forcing an election sooner than the 1980 date Somoza had set. But his only major contender, and arch-critic for twenty-five years, editor of the opposition newspaper *La Prensa*, the fifty-three-year-old Pedro Joaquin Chamorro was murdered on 10 January this year. The killing followed a campaign in *La Prensa* against a firm, Plasmaferesis, which is partly owned by Somoza, that traffics in selling Nicaraguan blood to American and European hospitals. Stories, perhaps exaggerated, were circulating in Managua that corpses found murdered by the death squads were also discovered to have been drained of blood.

Chamorro's murder set off a two-week general strike which was joined by the banks and association of small businessmen. A week earlier seven Roman Catholic bishops had denounced the régime for instituting a reign of terror, torture and greed, adding that they could no longer remain silent 'when a valuable sector of our people can see the taking up of arms as the only patriotic solution'. But again the United States government and Somoza's indubitable experience have been called upon to bail him out. As fighting in the streets continued two months after Chamorro's death, Terence Todman, the American Under Secretary of State for Latin American Affairs announced he hoped Nicaraguans would wait until the 1980 election. MacKenzie McCheyne have circulated yet another official version of these troubled affairs. And the Nicaraguan Ambassador to the United Nations has rebutted questions of torture. Let there be no mistake, Somoza is 'todo un caballero', 'a real gentleman', the ambassador said.

NIGER

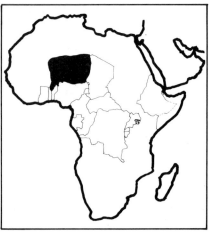

The 4.6 million people of Niger are really ruled by poverty and drought; the military junta by the French – the former colonialists who provide an army of technicians and are busy digging out the enormous uranium deposits conservatively estimated at 70,000 tons.

Lieutenant-Colonel Seynie Kountché, Head of State and President of the Supreme Military Council, seized power in a bloody coup in April 1974 and

Niger. Bororo tribe members watering their precious cattle, decimated by the Sahel drought

consolidated his position by a series of reshuffles, house arrests, dismissals of senior army officers, fierce fighting and a batch of life sentences for opponents which culminated in the execution of nine people two years later for their part in an attempted coup.

Kountché overthrew the civilian government of President Hamani Diori whose corruption and incompetence had become notorious. After the coup huge stocks of food sent as aid relief were discovered in ministers' houses and what had escaped to the people had only been made available, by government order, to those who paid income tax.

Very few do. Ninety-five per cent of the population live on a subsistence

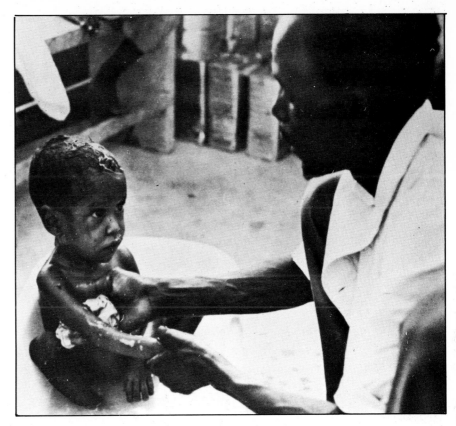

A bath being given – on doctor's prescription. Water is so scarce nomads seldom bathe

oasis, many have no income at all. Three-quarters of the vast semi-desert country (458,075 square miles) is too dry to support agriculture and the Sahel drought has virtually destroyed the centuries-old way of life of the Tuareg nomads. Tens of thousands of men, women, children and their precious camels have died. The beautiful cactus plants, the only green patches on the landscape, are poisonous, the water in the springs often too rich in minerals to drink.

Diori's indifference to his own people was made worse by muddled FAO bureaucracy and the totally inadequate transport system in the landlocked country. The British sent an observer to assess the extent of the famine but he was useless unless he was actually carrying food on his back. The people were so undernourished that common

Mercedes – the standard dictator's car.

Mercedes – the dictators' car as it often ends up

Like a pile of skulls – insect-damaged maize

diseases like measles were immediately fatal.

Diori's demise was heralded by a wave of strikes by young people which closed the schools and colleges for four months. After the coup he was imprisoned in a small three-roomed lodging at Zinder military camp and lingered on until he finally died, almost blind, in 1977.

Little seems to have changed since. The main export cash crop of ground-nuts had gone from 200,000 tons in 1972 to 100,000 in 1973 to an actual need to import in 1974. Kountché's army has brought with it first a plague of rats, then of locusts, which has led to a desperate world-wide appeal for food to overcome the shortfall in 1976.

The proud Tuareg have drifted into the towns looking for menial tasks like road-sweeping, but are being turned down. There has been no work. The oil crisis has made the trade deficit even more disastrous and the country is now propped up by foreign assistance. France, Canada, the United States and the UN have been building roads. But the French-controlled SOMAIR mining company has now been joined by German and Japanese companies and the government itself to exploit the uranium. By 1980 production is hoped to be at least 5,000 tons a year.

PAKISTAN

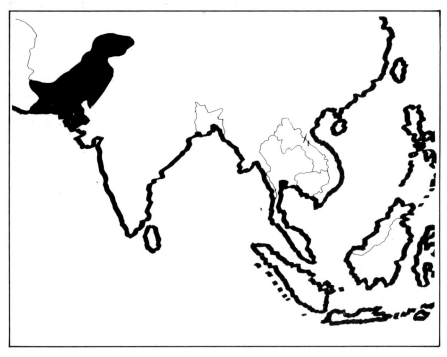

Pakistan, with an estimated population of eighty million, used to be one of the world's largest democracies. Until July 1977, when General Mohammed Zia-ul-Haq grew tired of the politicians, arrested them all, and promised a '90-day operation' to put the country back on a democratic footing. His timing has proved slightly out.

Nobody shed any tears at the coup. The only wetness in anybody's eyes was put down to an unusually violent monsoon.

The former Prime Minister, Mr Ali Bhutto, had only himself to blame. By March 1978 he had fallen about as low as he could. He had been condemned to death.

Bhutto was never a modest man. 'My crime is that this country has never produced a leader of my calibre,' he said three months before he was toppled. He was regarded as a brilliant, if ruthless, leader, with his background of excellent degrees in law and political science from Oxford and Berkeley, California. His Gucci footwear and Huddersfield cloth made up in Savile Row scored him sartorial points with the leaders as diverse as those of US and China whom he courted. But they did little else to help him at home.

Bhutto surprised everyone in 1977 by suddenly calling national and provincial elections for March to counter the increasing agitation from the opposition.

He made a severe mistake. His opponents unexpectedly banded together to form the nine-factor Pakistan National Alliance. The unlikely combination of diverse elements had one single unifying factor – they hated him.

The result of the election was landslide for Bhutto's Pakistan People's Party, followed by an outcry against massive vote-rigging by his own supporters. It was probably unnecessary, as he would have won anyhow, and it started him on the slippery slope.

Agitation followed, and he was forced to negotiate with the nine leaders through the bars of the prisons he had thrown them into. Accusing the US of financing a campaign to unseat him he finally yielded to demands for fresh elections, presumably designed to take place without such blatant expedients as the last time.

He then foolishly departed for a triumphant and money-raising tour of six Islamic countries, leaving further negotiations to his Finance Minister, a heavy-handed individual who only increased the opposition suspicions that the entire programme was an exercise in insincerity.

The Army, which had ruled the country for thirteen years previous to

The state airline – modern Boeings provided by modern loans

General Zia-ul-Haq. Ninety days is a long time in politics

Bhutto's assumption of the presidency in December 1971, was by now becoming increasingly fed up with shooting its fellow Punjabis who insisted on demonstrating. In its eyes the confrontation between the politicians had reached a deadlock, paralysed the country, and cost an immediate estimate of 750 million US dollars to the already hopelessly lop-sided economy.

Bhutto had made a further mistake in promoting the diminutive, polo-playing General Zia, who seven years earlier had commanded nothing larger than a brigade. Now Chief of Staff, he moved his High Command. Bhutto was taken away to a Himalayan hill-station twenty miles from his superb residence in the capital where General Zia stayed – in his similar mansion, 200 yards down the road.

The Army stated it would end the agitation, the vindictiveness and corruption of Bhutto's régime, and alter a situation which had led to the imposition of martial law in three major cities.

General Zia was declared Chief Martial Law Administrator. He declared he had no political ambitions. It is best not to in Pakistan. The previous military leader, General Yahya Khan, had taken a short-cut to disaster through the civil war which led to the formation of Bangladesh in 1971. Zia was quite firm that Pakistan would return to civilian rule for the third time.

He startled the world by his programme. The former member of the British Indian Army Scouts, forgetting his training, promptly returned the country's legal system to the Middle Ages by imposing a system of punishments including amputation of the left hand, public flogging and death sentences. The amputations, following the Muslim code practised in Libya, had to be carried out by a qualified surgeon using an anaesthetic. Amputation was for banditry or theft. Crimes such as political activity of any kind merely carried sentences of five years or a whipping.

The democratic time-table fell to pieces. The elections on the ninety-day schedule were first cancelled, then followed up in 1978 by a law negating the tea parties, religious gatherings and village meetings which had been used for surreptitious political activity since the supposed date of the vote.

Any function where a banner was raised or a political slogan put up now rendered its members liable to seven years and between five and twenty lashes.

The economy, where twenty families are said to control sixty per cent of the country's industrial assets, had crumbled even further. By December 1977 the trade deficit had widened to 100 million US dollars a month. Zia led a campaign of abuse and vilification against shopkeepers, accusing them of hoarding and black-marketeering. A series of measures to try to alleviate the situation failed. After the coup, Zia went to Saudi Arabia, Iran and Kuwait for funds, but returned with nothing except

The rush-hour – when there is no curfew

a short-term loan from Kuwait. After more overseas tours he announced that he had raised 400 million US dollars in firm pledges, mostly from Saudi Arabia. Iran could not help because of its static oil revenue and own development needs, so he hoped instead that it would delay repayment of the first instalment of a 580 million US dollar loan already given to his country.

The Khyber Pass near Peshawar, now the gateway to a military dictatorship

The vast majority of his people meanwhile continued to earn less than £40 per head per annum – about the price of each of Bhutto's silk shirts, hand-made in Jermyn Street, London.

By March 1978 Bhutto was forced to ponder which one he would wear for his execution. He was tried for various minor offences of misappropriating funds, violating land reforms and misusing his position, but more seriously had been found guilty on the major accusation of complicity in the murder of one of his father's most bitter enemies four years previously.

His tortuous protestations about the way the trial was conducted went unheeded.

In a 100-page affidavit he detailed his criticisms. The Chief Justice was holding a government post apart from his judicial duties; he was tried in a small bare concreted room in prison; the motives of the witnesses were questionable, etc. The trial, he alleged, had been a five-month-long legal charade. Nobody took any notice of his document because they were not allowed to read it. The press was forbidden to print it, and instead continued the propaganda campaign against him which had run alongside the hearings.

Ignoring a warning from his daughter that the rivers of Pakistan would flow with blood if anything happened to him, the court announced its verdict. He was to be hanged, obviously too dangerous to be allowed to remain in circulation like Mrs Gandhi, and like her to have growing support when he was out of power rather than in it.

What has happened since has basically stemmed from that decision.

World aid. Allahdad opening a ditch to his five-acre farm under a scheme financed by the World Bank

PARAGUAY

President Stroessner. The son of a
Bavarian brewer, advised by Nazis
in hiding and the CIA

General Alfredo Stroessner, the sixty-four-year-old son of an immigrant Bavarian brewer, has run the tightest little dictatorship in Latin America since his faction of the army took over twenty-four years ago.

According to Amnesty International, in Paraguay 'all individual rights may be suppressed if a state of emergency is declared. President Stroessner has proclaimed states of emergency at three-monthly intervals since 1954, lifting them only on election days and alleging the threat of communist subversion.' This year he has been right on form. In February 1977 delegates for a constitutional convention were elected to sweep aside the restriction on the president's being elected for another term. The only votes cast were for the official government Colorado party. Not one opposition poster challenged the mammoth neon sign over the capital, Asunción's, main square proclaiming 'Peace, Work and Welfare with Stroessner'.

Early this year Stroessner was re-elected, for another six years, as usual.

It seems odd that Jimmy Carter has excluded Paraguay from his much vaunted list of countries which systematically deny human rights. In Paraguay (national motto – 'By reason or by force') Supreme Court members belong to the ruling party and are appointed by Stroessner himself. Only once during his rule has one judge dared dissent from the usual unanimous rejection of habeas-corpus writs. That was in connection with the arrest of the Liberal Radical party leader, Efren Gonzalez. The errant judge was immediately dismissed.

Stroessner also has the singular distinction of filling his gaols not just with Communists (whose leaders languished in prison from 1958 until last year when they were released only to be cornered now in the Peruvian Embassy where they sought asylum), members of the sporadic and fragile opposition parties, and impoverished peasants who have spoken out. He locks up 'problematic elements' of his own Colorado party as well. Again, according to Amnesty International: 'Middle ranking officers and militants may be held for a number of years, while more prominent figures may secure their own release after a short prison term by renewed avowals of loyalty, or by deportation.' Among them are 800 members who were said to be plotting a coup in 1975.

For good measure, Amnesty reports, 'relations are taken as hostage pending appearance of the wanted dissident, or as punishment, or to ensure everyone remains silent when the men in the family have been assassinated.'

There should be no mistake about prison conditions in arguably the worst dungeons in the world. There are reports that clothes are hung from the roofs to make room to sit and lie down. Tin cans and pails used for toilets are emptied only every few days. Men are tied by ankle-chains to the wall and to each other, in some cases for more than a year at a time. They are often subjected

to cold baths in winter in the dark. In one camp, Tacumbu, prisoners break stones twelve hours a day, Sundays and public holidays included, live in huts where they sleep and eat on the floor, surviving on starvation diets. There are no doctors. Preferred tortures are the 'el sargento' – a cat of nine tails with lead balls at the tips of the thongs – and the submerging until near drowning of prisoners in baths of human excrement, in addition to prolonged beatings and burnings with hot iron bars. Many prisoners simply 'disappear' and relatives never hear of them again. The security forces were in part trained by escaped Nazis and SS guards. More recently 'specialists' from the CIA have been introducing 'more sophisticated' psychological methods, including drugs.

Stroessner sent troops to join the US marines after they had landed in the Dominican Republic in 1965, and offered to send 'volunteers' to fight in Vietnam. At home, the country has never fully recovered from its disastrous defeat by the Brazilians, Uruguayans and Argentinians, 1865–70, when over half the country's population was killed.

Such is the economic development of Paraguay, that there are dirt roads outside the Presidential Palace
Camera Press

People were starving, even the generals went barefoot. Their only reasonably successful foreign venture was a war with Bolivia, in the 1930s, the Chaco war, largely motivated by Standard Oil of New Jersey's desire to start drilling oil wells in disputed border territory.

Six hundred thousand of Paraguay's less than three million citizens now live in the slums of Buenos Aires and anywhere else they can get to. There are 40,000 indigenous Indians who have no rights at all. It is still common, according to a high-ranking British Embassy official, to drive out onto the grasslands in the north of the country and shoot them on sight. 'It's like the Wild West up there,' he recently told a meeting of London bankers.

The Indians have been corralled into barbed-wire reservations from where the children are sold into slavery to grow up as servants in Asunción. This leaves law-abiding Paraguayans free to pursue their daily affairs – the most widespread of which is large-scale smuggling of contraband drugs, and luxury goods.

Most of America's heroin used to pass through Asunción. Now, next to Hong Kong, it is the world's largest centre for illicit cigarettes and whisky, willingly supplied to other Latin American régimes.

But Stroessner's law enforcement officers have the situation well in control. In 1973, the British manager of Brooke Bond Oxo's Paraguayan ranches mysteriously disappeared in Asunción. He was freed after a week following a gun battle in which two men guarding him were killed. Though they were originally said to be Argentinian left-wing guerillas, it soon emerged that Brooke Bond's man was but a pawn in an inter-Paraguayan security service feud. The most reliable sources suggest that the police chief, Pastor Coronel, suspected that the Minister of Interior, Dr Sabino Augusto Montanaro, had revealed to an American magazine that Coronel and the commander of the Paraguayan cavalry, General Andres Rodriguez, controlled the narcotics trade. So Coronel neatly encouraged some of Montanaro's relatives and henchmen to kidnap the hapless Britisher and demand a ransom. Which of course Brooke Bond refused to pay. Instead, Coronel quickly solved the crime, and Brooke Bond paid, reportedly, £150,000 into the police benevolent fund. Asunción society was pleased to read recently that General Rodriguez's daughter has agreed to give her hand in marriage to Stroessner's son.

Visitors to Asunción report that virtually every conceivable form of contraband is still freely available in the open street market stalls. Small children are said to be employed by the 'smugglers' to ride on the top of the tarpaulined lorries rushing from the quay through the town in order to discourage ambushes from other well-organized armed gangs eager to hijack their rivals' deals.

President Stroessner, of course, has had no time to pronounce his views on these affairs. He is keeping himself busy bartering with Argentina and Brazil over hydro-electric dams on the coun-tries' mutual river borders, negotiating with oil companies and Brazilian bankers who have been buying up large tracts of eastern and northern Paraguay, where Indians once lived, for commercial farms. The area of a recent oil find in the north has been surrounded with barbed wire and declared a military zone. Stroessner has also been actively advancing his reputation as providing a possible safe haven for Latin dictators who may be deposed, much as he welcomed fleeing Nazis. The Bolivians and Uruguayans, among others, are said to have borne this in mind. So too has the United States, which reportedly is seriously considering investing hundreds of millions of dollars in strategic military bases in case the Argentinian and Chilean juntas should fall. Confidence was running so high that in March 1977 Stroessner hosted a jamboree for the 'Latin American Anti-Communist Confederation'. Aside from the bosses of nearly every torturer and hangman on

In the nineteenth century Paraguay was the most prosperous country in southern Latin America

the continent, there were delegations from Taiwan, Zaire, Croatian nationalists, South Africans and hard line American cold warriors, all come to hear about Marxist infiltration in high places. The Pope, it was agreed, is but the puppet of Marxist cardinals.

The Paraguayan Law for the Defence of Public Peace and Liberty of Persons officially provides for a three- to five-year prison sentence for anyone who proposes 'to destroy violently the republican and democratic régime of the nation'. Every evening as the sun sets in the Plaza Constitucion the national flag is lowered, trumpets sounded and citizens spontaneously rise to attention. Patriotism, at moments like this, knows few bounds.

Recently Stroessner escorted a prominent visiting dignitary to the airport. When they arrived at the awaiting plane, the life-President promptly unzipped his flies and peed on the plane's wheel. His guard, a colonel, smartly jumped to attention, and nudging the dignitary, exclaimed, 'What a democrat – our President!'

The biggest trade in Paraguay is smuggling. The contraband goes to all of South America

PHILIPPINES

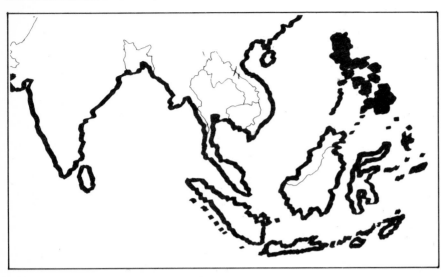

President Marcos. The playboy of
South-East Asia *Gamma*

It has been six years since President Ferdinand Marcos declared martial law. Six years since students occupying the university broadcast for three days over the campus radio a looped tape recording that had been secretly made, of El Presidente hoarsely demanding an American starlet make love with him. The security forces were buckled with laughter as they tried to restore order. The President's machismo and personalized CIA bulletproof vest are much discussed on Manila's off-shore gambling ship – a business which Marcos's wife, Imelda, closely follows. Marcos's fortune, his homes in Switzerland and Chelsea, his control over virtually all major government contracts also intrigue visitors to the Philippines, struck by the fourteen brand new and near empty hotels around Manila Bay built to impress one of his main creditors, the World Bank-IMF. Imelda, the rags-to-riches former beauty queen who nonetheless claims to be descended from Spanish nobility, is Governor of the city.

The *Daily Express*, Manila's main newspaper which Marcos owns, on the other hand attempts to direct attention more to the Mariveles Free Trade Zone, a mammoth tax-free industrial development site just outside Manila built on property which, once again, was part of the Marcos estate.

'We love the multi-nationals,' Marcos said. And there the multi-nationals are offered what advertisements boast is the best deal in all South-East Asia – tax holidays, repatriation of profits, allowances and guaranteed low wages. Strikes are banned, unions are under firm government control, and the minimum wage is below the family subsistence level according to the government's statistics. Following Ford, Volkswagen, British Leyland, Chrysler, Sony, General Electric and Phillips are all moving there. Marcos also offers multi-nationals liberal environment controls, and Kawasaki will soon have a massive steel mill spewing out pollutants which the Japanese government has banned as highly carcinogenic. Del Monte, Standard Fruit, Firestone, Goodrich and Goodyear have for years maintained sugar, pineapple and rubber plantations in the southern Philippines, many of which are far larger in acreage than is normally allowed under Philippine law.

Since granted independence by the United States in 1946, the country has been run by gangsters and men whom the United States has kept in power. The most manipulable of Marcos's predecessors, Ramon Magsaysay, was a strike-breaker. General Edward G. Landsdale, previously a Madison Avenue advertising executive, virtually resur-

Bananas for American supermarkets, from closely guarded plantations

rected Magsaysay and stood by his side throughout his term. Literally. He had a desk in Magsaysay's office, and a cot in his bedroom.

Marcos won the 1966 presidential election on his reputation as a lover, war hero and big spender. In 1969 he won an unprecedented second term after a campaign during which treasury funds were so heavily drawn upon that the peso had to be devalued soon after. But the only way to be sure of remaining president after his second term expired in November 1973 was to declare martial law. Which he did on 21 September 1972, following an announced assassination attempt on his defence secretary. 'Only a passing phase,' Marcos said.

Cockfighting is popular in the Philippines, as are all types of gambling

He abolished the legislature, suspended habeas-corpus. And 30,000 people, including the leader of the opposition Liberal Party, Senator Benigno Aquino, were arrested. Military courts were set up, arms confiscated, and the whole bureaucracy asked to resign. Posters suddenly appeared throughout the country pronouncing a 'New Society', calling for discipline and praising the 'revolution from the centre'. Filipino businessmen say Marcos simply centralized the bribes. Nonetheless somewhere between six and twenty thousand political prisoners are still in gaol.

At one of Marcos's heavily staged referenda in October 1976, fifteen Catholic bishops spoke out: 'The only palpable fact is that martial law is a régime of coercion and fear, of institutionalized manipulation and deception.' Both Amnesty International and American clergymen found torture is used, despite Marcos's protestations to the contrary.

The 'cranker dynamo' is the favoured

device. Wires from a ninety-volt hand-cranked field telephone are attached to a person's fingers and sex organs. When the crank is turned, they scream, which is why they are 'interrogated' in 'safe houses' detached from the main prison blocks. They are also beaten, kicked and burned.

In 1976 Marcos suffered a serious blow. He went to the Nairobi conference of non-aligned states expecting the sort of reception he is accustomed to at home. He didn't get it. Since then Imelda has become a roving ambassador, visiting China, Havana and Tripoli and bringing back 'good ideas' which are immediately put into effect. The police can now be seen pushing harried Manilan pedestrians into rough queues, and office workers have been enjoined to take a week's vacation working with farmers, all part of the 'New Society'.

In the southern Philippines Marcos is fighting a war against Muslim separatists who have tied up most of his army and have been draining the treasury for years. Now he is trying to starve them out through a policy euphemistically called 'resource control', whereby families are entitled to only three kilos of rice a day and need military permits to buy nails, batteries and medicines. The army has declared vast areas 'free fire zones', meaning the villages are now, officially, battlefields. The expedient of 'destroying towns [with napalm] to save them from the guerillas' is reportedly widespread. The United States closely follows the war, because it trained much of the Philippine army, and because its only major bases in South-East Asia following withdrawal from Thailand in 1976 are there.

The Clark Air Force base covers a larger area than all US air bases outside the continental United States. The bars and brothels which begin a few hundred

These Muslim separatists have been fighting the Philippines Army for years. Their families support them *Gamma*

The United States equips the Filipino police. Before the First World War, American Marines killed over 300,000 Filipino nationalists

Marcos and the 'lovely' Imelda, his wife, whose 'good ideas' are instantly put into effect

yards outside its main gate extend for over two miles along the Philippine National Highway. The Subic Naval base services the US Pacific Fleet. Over ten per cent of the population of Olongapo, the city next door, are prostitutes. The two bases together are the country's second largest employer after the government.

Major-General Fidel Ramos, Chief of Staff of the Armed Forces, Chief of the Philippines Constabulary, and Director General of the Integrated National Police – and Marcos's nephew – trained at West Point, Fort Bragg and Fort Benning in the United States. Even the Manila police are equipped by American firms. But most of the forty-three million Filipinos, living on the country's over 7,000 islands, are too busy struggling to survive on small plots of land to pay much attention to Marcos's foreign affairs. According to economists, while the Gross National Product continues to grow, the overall standard of living is falling, so much so that Filipinos now eat, per capita, fewer calories of nourishment each day than the people of India.

Last year Marcos announced that an Interum Batasang Pambansa (Legislative Assembly) would be elected this year. As the campaign began, former Senator Aquino, in prison facing a death sentence, declared he would run from gaol. Marcos briefly toured villages accompanied by contingents of heavily armed guards reminding people, 'There is no short cut to normalization of our political life.'

Under the Philippines' various constitutions, Marcos automatically becomes Prime Minister of the assembly while remaining President, adding further to his powers, one being to overrule all assembly deliberations, as usual, by his own decree.

THAILAND

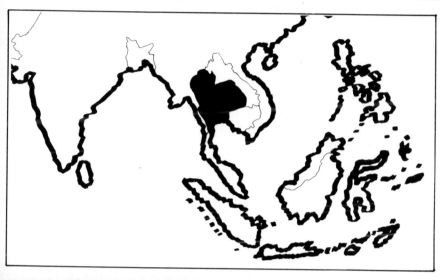

'One of the major factors which recommends Thailand to the investor over the other countries in the region is its abundant supply of cheap and trainable labour. The minimum wage for unskilled labour in the Bangkok metropolis was fixed at 25 baht per day (1.25 dollars) . . . Outside Bangkok the minimum wage has been set at 16 baht.'

Fifteen powerful reasons why you should invest in Thailand, published by the Thai Board of Investment

On 6 October 1976, Thailand underwent what was probably the world's most widely expected coup. At seven in the morning Border Patrol Police accompanied by paramilitary 'Village Scouts' stormed Thammasat University in Bangkok and slaughtered the students who were accused of insulting the Crown Prince Vajiralongkorn. The Border Police are United States trained and financed, with money for weapons provided through the American International Narcotics Control Program. The 'Village Scouts' enjoy Thai royal patronage, and are trained by security experts. After butchering the students they marched to the government house where, as if from nowhere, the Crown Prince appeared dressed in his army captain's uniform to address the mob. He praised their 'bravery and devotion to the nation' and told them to disperse. A twenty-four-man military junta seized power, declaring martial law, so ending the only democratic period in Thai history since the absolute monarchy had to concede power to the military in 1932.

A Buddhist monk answered the question as to whether it was a transgression to kill communist and student activists. 'Yes,' he said, 'but only a small one when compared to the good of defending the nation, king and religion.' Over one

General Kriangsak, head of the Thailand dictatorship. He fought with the United States in the Korean War

million books were burned, including copies of George Orwell's *Animal Farm*. Such was Thailand's return to traditional rule. Three thousand students were held in Bangkok's overcrowded gaols. Charity workers collected nearly 300 corpses, not including those who drowned while trying to escape. Thousands fled to join the guerillas in the countryside.

The next year was a binge of corruption, overspending and repression unequalled in Thailand even during the Vietnam war. King Bhumibol was pleased that cement imports were restricted, as he is the major shareholder in the Siam Cement Company. There was a record trade deficit, rice production plummeted, the standard of living fell, and forty per cent of the government budget was spent by the Departments of Defence and Interior. The latter employs half a million people alone.

So on 20 October 1977 there was another coup, this time led by pipe-smoking General Kriangsak Chamanand who declared himself 'National Peacekeeper' and took over as Premier and Minister of the Interior as well as Supreme Commander of the Armed Forces.

The cement duty is down, the king celebrated his fiftieth birthday by releasing 10,000 prisoners and reducing the sentences of 30,000 others. And the Revolutionary Council insisted that all Royal memos and decrees have to be countersigned. Kriangsak also allowed gaoled student leaders to have legal counsel, and promised elections for a purely formal national assembly later this year.

Without these measures the generals stand little chance of defeating the nationalist and communist insurgents who range over vast areas of the Thai countryside.

Kriangsak made amends with the

The Thammasat massacre. Paid right-wing agitators played with student corpses

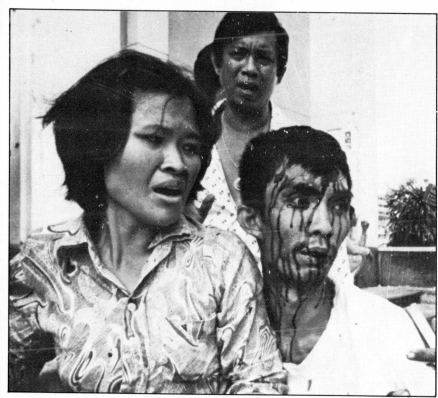

6 October 1976. The Thammasat massacre. These students were lucky still to be alive

Chinese and Cambodians. But his army and the Border Police have been doing poorly against the guerillas, even with considerable help from American Vietnam veterans and British-trained Malaysian troops. Daily, people in Bangkok play an amusing game of trying to reconcile what they read of the army's exploits in the heavily censored press and what they hear over the illegal liberation radio. Over 8,000 people have been arrested, according to the *New York Times*, mostly near Bangkok as 'threats to the security of the state.'

'How to tell a liberated area in Thailand,' a Thai Internal Security Organizations Command Manual reads: 'If rustlers disappear, gambling dies, hooligans reform and drug addicts

The army rules in Bangkok

The United States is supplying more arms to Thailand than during the Vietnam war

kick the habit; if demand for books, paper and pencils and toothpaste and soap suddenly increases; and if public sanitation and order improve, then the village is communist-infested and should be destroyed.'

Most of the forty-two million Thais are perpetually in debt to landlords and banks who sell the rice they produce at well over four times what they are nominally paid.

There are estimated to be 300,000 prostitutes in Bangkok ('City of Angels') now servicing Japanese businessmen in the hotels, brothels and strip-clubs through which American GIs once prowled. Thailand's 400,000 heroin addicts are supplied by rackets set up by

Unemployed peasants' sons are offered jobs, clothes and money by the army. Their officers expect hefty bribes

generals and American agents who cornered much of the opium market during the Vietnam war, and who can now be seen banging into each others' Mercedes Benzes in Bangkok traffic jams.

Several attempts have been made to assassinate the king. Nonetheless S. Woodrow Spoonauggle, the President of the Thai Chamber of Commerce, has gone to great lengths to reassure multinational corporations that General Kriangsak is the right man to be in charge. He won the American Order of Merit during the Korean war, trained at Fort Leavenworth, Kansas, and fought with CIA-backed Thai mercenaries in Laos.

The United States made Thailand a massive military base during the Vietnam war. They also put as many Thais in uniform as they could find and equipped them with .30 calibre high-velocity assault rifles, machine-guns, mortars, grenade launchers and tanks. But this is dwarfed by the scale on which the United States is arming the Thai junta now. In 1976 they sold Thailand over 100 million dollars' worth of arms, more than the total sales for the previous twenty-five years. The Carter administration has increased sales further – all so Kriangsak can try to 'pacify' the countryside now he and other generals have already destroyed the country's democratic institutions by coups.

Thousands of students and young people have fled to join the guerillas in the countryside, rather than risk life in Bangkok

TOGO

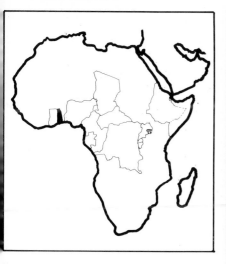

'With his athletic build, supple bearing, sparkling smile, General Gnassingbé Eyadéma is a force of nature', read a full-page advertisement in *The Times* on 13 January 1976, 'his favourite pastime is still hunting and, like Edward VII of England, he is one of the world's best shots.'

Eyadéma did not shoot anybody when he took over his small country exactly nine years previously. The coup was bloodless, and since then he has remained in power by using his favourite tactic of threatening to resign and being dissuaded by 'spontaneous demonstrations' which bear a curious resemblance to the 1930s, when German military occupiers taught the school-children to sing the German national anthem word perfect.

The Togo government explains: 'Three days after the restatement of his desire to step down in 1971 a large crowd encircled the military camp in a monster demonstration to demand that he remain as Head of State and from all corners of the country messages of support flowed in. President Eyadéma accepted that this was truly the will of his people and, whilst maintaining a camaraderie with all the Togolese, he,

by popular acclaim, continued to hold the office as Head of State and is proud to do so.'

He is 'an easy and approachable man listening with equal attention to all the people . . . The most striking things about him are integrity and uprightness

combined with a goodness which is the sign of true greatness . . . self-motivated he has avoided the airy-fairy intellectual path.' He lives in a military compound, 'preferring camp life to the pomp and circumstance of the Presidential palace'.

Occasionally he strolls the streets of

'Giant maniac machines' – phosphate mining

Lomé, the capital, 'to take the temperature of the people'.

His military coup is justified on the grounds that political parties were 'no more than the seat of dissension and discord'. They have therefore been dissolved. Instead 'a movement – not a party – of national unity' has been formed, the Rassemblement du Peuple Togolais. 'This is a very popular movement – its members include almost all the Togo people.'

For the past eleven years Eyadéma has built a massive personality cult. His name is incessantly repeated on the state radio as he exhorts the peasants to greater efforts, or is effusively thanked

Delights for the tourist

for his services to the nation. His face stares from thousands of billboards and every village has massed troupes of political singers and dancers, in outfits emblazoned with his portrait, who chant his praises.

Togo, sandwiched between Ghana and Benin, has a festering border dispute over the fate of the Ewe people, whose territory was chopped in half by the arbitrary division of the former German colony into British administrative area (Ghana) and French (Togo).

The government has a scathing view of the former rulers: 'In the anachronistic first decade of the twentieth century a Reich Kommissar was stomping the great wharf at Lomé . . . Like Ozymandias the Imperial jetty is crumbled and smashed, whilst the French successor lies derelict alongside.'

Since then Eyadéma has been pulling in aid from wherever he can, pushing a campaign of national authenticity, and nationalizing the French mining company getting out the phosphates which form the basis of the economy, using 'giant maniac machines which bite out great mouthfuls'.

In 1974 he survived a mysterious plane crash which he claimed had been engineered by the mining company, and assumed the unofficial title of the 'Immortal One'. The site has now become a place of annual national pilgrimage.

Eyadéma is trying to attract tourists to enjoy the delights of – for example – the Benin 'hotel in the grand manner, more of a Metropole at Brighton'. They are invited to go 'night-clubbing at the Pussy Cat or just prowling around enjoying the tropical night . . . The police strike just about the perfect balance of firmness and efficiency.'

Meanwhile Amnesty International has reported torture of political detainees, as much for the guards' entertainment as for information, and has the names of twenty people who reportedly died under interrogation. They have been forced to beat each other with chains and whips. The government has claimed that there are now no political prisoners and invited Amnesty to inspect the gaols in 1977. When it wrote about the invitation there was no reply.

Eyadéma has also had coup attempts, including a botched plot masterminded by a mysterious Canadian arms dealer in October 1977. The dealer recruited British mercenaries, including ex-SAS men and a serving British Army NCO, but the 'Dirty Dozen' were foiled by the British Foreign Office, which tipped Eyadéma off via the country's American ambassador.

'My people love me as kind friend,' he told a British reporter who went there afterwards and watched goats mingling with officers on his parade ground. 'Why should anybody try to kill me?'

Street scene in the capital, Lomé

129

UGANDA

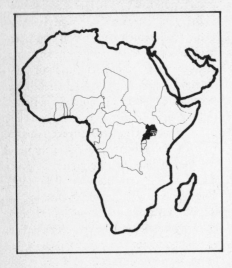

Black mood – Amin at the UN 1975
Gamma

President Idi Amin is the world's best-known military tyrant. He is also one of the bloodiest, imposing his erratic will through his alien mercenaries and propped up by a combination of Arab money, sales of his coffee (biggest purchaser the USA), and the British government, which welcomed him so warmly to start with and has not yet stopped the twice weekly 'whisky run' from Stansted airport, Essex, which keeps his henchmen in the goodies they demand.

Amin has made himself infamous by a series of brutal killings and wholesale massacres. The number of dead since he took over from President Milton Obote with his military coup on 25 January 1971 is impossible to estimate reliably. Figures vary between 50,000 and 300,000. Amin has become a by-word for his clumsy and botched attempts to cover up murders like that of the Catholic Archbishop Janun Luwuum, who was machine-gunned to death and then supposed to have died in a fake car accident. Or the equally inept and blatant lie that Mrs Dora Bloch was on the PLO hijacked aircraft which Israeli commandos freed in the Entebbe raid. This raid gave a true estimate of Amin's strength. When the

commandos arrived all Amin's army chiefs promptly hid and he himself, shortly back from Mauritius, so completely failed to understand the position, he thought it was an attempted coup by his own men.

Many people cannot understand why this nearly illiterate man, who has bankrupted his country and destroyed its economy by the expulsion of the 45,000 Ugandan Asians, is still in power. Since then it is estimated that 300,000 of the middle class have fled. The Asians were expelled in 1972 at ninety days' notice by Amin on what he described as 'God's instructions' which had come to him in a dream. Their bank accounts were frozen, they were given a $100 US allowance, and their belongings taken to the airport 'to be sent on after them'. They were looted by the army. The businesses were then parcelled out ad hoc to people who had no idea how to run them. One man, given a clothes store, sold the shirts on the basis of the collar size, thinking that was the price. When all the goods had gone the shops were boarded up.

The expulsion of the Asians, although Amin was astonished by the effect it had on his economy, showed how clever and wily he is at dealing with his own people. The Asians were unpopular – they had been called the Jews of Africa – and his move was seen as a blow for the native people. His farcical attempts at world diplomacy – the 'Save Britain Fund' launched in December 1973, his offers to mediate in the Scottish devolution debate, or his telegram to Nixon wishing him a 'speedy recovery' from Watergate, or to Ford – 'I love you' – are taken seriously by many of his own people, who genuinely believe that he is a great world leader, able to talk to other heads of state just by picking up the telephone. The impression is of course fostered by his complete control over all the media.

He also has enormous personal presence, with his flamboyance, ebullience and sexual prowess (women quite genuinely make themselves available to

him). In his early days he soon abandoned all pretext of government on paper, helicoptering round the country and making airy promises of hospitals, etc., which his hapless ministers would then jot down. Later he started announcing new plans on the radio, and ministers had to listen constantly to find out what they were supposed to do.

All pretence of actual government, never mind the 'honest, fair and completely fair elections' which he promised on seizing power, has long since been abandoned. Ministers are mere ciphers, and power rests entirely with his alien mercenaries, the 'Nubians' – Southern Sudanese – and the members of his own Kakwa tribe, who have negligible official salaries and live off the loot he parcels out to them. With no families or possessions they are expected to flee when his régime is finally toppled.

Ugandan villages offer nothing more than subsistence living. The young are drifting to the towns

If they can reach the border they will survive.

The Nubians are Muslims, which fits in well with Amin's pretence of turning Uganda into a Muslim state. He has banned twenty-seven churches, including the Salvation Army. The pretence enables him to pull in money from Arab countries, particularly his close friend Colonel Qadhafi of Libya, where he keeps a country residence.

The mercenaries are for the dreaded 'State Research Bureau', his 2,000-

Public execution supervised by Amin, 1973. Watched by 30,000 most of whom could not read the advertisement, 'For a longer and better life' *Gamma*

132

horribly mutilated and tortured. A foreign service officer had his eyes gouged out, his genitals cut off and was partially skinned before his body was dumped. Others have been run over by tanks at the military barracks. One nurse has told how she was ordered to decapitate six bodies, and spray the heads with preservatives so they could be taken to Amin for his own 'fun'.

An example of his utter lack of humanity was the death of his second wife Kay, whom he had divorced. She was found dismembered in the boot of a car. He ordered the corpse to be sewn back together, wheeled it out of the mortuary and showed it to her three children, aged between four and eight. 'Your mother was a bad woman,' he shouted at them. 'See what has happened to her.' Two of the various women whom Amin wanted had their lovers murdered. He is currently married to two wives, the second known as 'Suicide' Sarah. She used to be a go-go dancer with a band formed by the Revolutionary Suicide Mechanized Regiment of the Army.

Amin's main method of corpse disposal, after the victims have been bundled into the boots of cars by his 'spooks', is to throw them into the river. Sometimes they are dropped from helicopters. The crocodiles are then supposed to eat them. Because this method is relatively inefficient he employs a full-time boatman to pull the puffed and bloated corpses out of the water above the Owen Falls dam on the Nile.

Amin has personally been proven guilty of murder by international bodies, and has publicly stated that human flesh is saltier than leopard meat. He is known to consult witch-doctors.

One of the reasons he has lasted so long is the engaging façade of the relaxed and simple man he puts forward to visitors, receiving them in the office where according to latest reports he still keeps a portrait of the Queen on the wall. He also particularly likes the

Tea plantations – one of the sources of revenue that keep Amin in power

strong 'personal bodyguard', which publicly and frequently drags away people for execution.

The cowed population turns a blind eye when these thugs in their flowered shirts and bell-bottomed trousers re-move or machine-gun people from public places like streets and restaurants.

The SRB is backed up by the Military Police and the Public Safety Unit, to form a total force of about 15,000 men. The atrocities they have committed are innumerable. Before they die, men, women and children are often

Kampala. Slums, modern buildings, terror and wholesale execution

jet which is on permanent stand-by ready for a coup.

His mercenaries meanwhile have to be kept happy as there is a lot less to loot than there used to be. This is done through Britain by the Stansted flights. A company called Lebel (East Africa), operating from Wardour Street in Soho, buys everything he needs for cash. Dozens of British companies are still doing business with him. In the first two months of 1977 alone he bought £1.9 million worth of British goods.

The items on the 'whisky run' give an idea of what life is like in Kampala. They range from Mercedes through machines with obvious military potential like Land-Rovers to crates of Scotch, cigarettes, breeding cattle, suits, steaks, Coca-Cola and toilet rolls. Butter is £5 a pound in the capital, salt often unavailable, and the people so frightened they dare not have relatives round for their poor meals in case it is interpreted as conspiracy.

In 1976 Amin exported £32.4 million in goods to the UK and bought back £11.2 million for his own country. Attempts have been made to stop trade with Uganda, and particularly the Stansted flights, but so far they have failed. The only real move was in September 1977 when the NAAFI, under public pressure, stopped their contract to supply his armed forces with alcohol, tobacco, food and clothing. The contract, worked out of Nairobi, was worth £1 million a year.

Meanwhile he remains in power. His agents use methods like the sledge-hammer death routine, in which one prisoner is promised a reprieve if he batters his fellow to death. The same promise is then made to a third man about him, and so it goes on. He supplements these private murders with public executions watched by crowds of thousands.

In an attempt to improve his international image, he has declared 1978 'a year of peace, love, unity and reconciliation'.

Scots and admires the bagpipes. It is only after they have gone that he gives orders like 'Give him the VIP treatment' – torture before execution – and which are carefully not recorded in writing so there is no evidence to be used against him.

He has been helped, despite his nose-diving economy, by the soaring world price of coffee, his main cash crop, and for which the US is the main buyer. In November 1977 the trade to America was valued at 200 million dollars a year; another 150 million dollars' worth goes to other European countries. Attempts have been made to boycott the trade, but the American government is really awaiting an upturn of the Brazilian crop.

The Arabs keep him supplied with hard cash, which he throws out in bundles. It means nothing to him – he has been unable to understand why a country cannot just print as many bank-notes as it likes. At the same time he has large hoards of foreign currency stacked abroad in case he has to flee in the

URUGUAY

'The biggest torture chamber in Latin America'
Senator Frank Church, USA

Uruguay is ruled by decrees issued by generals and admirals sitting on a National Security Council, and a septuagenarian right-wing lawyer, Dr Aparicio Méndez, whom they co-opted as President and who will stay in office only as long as they please. Parliament is abolished, trade unions banned, the press is totally censored, as part of the programme of 'purified democracy'. Members of the old political parties have been deprived of all political rights for fifteen years. Civil servants have lost tenure, so they can be sacked immediately, and judges have to be approved by the generals.

Under a proposed 'state of dangerousness' decree people can be sent to gaol for ten years or exiled purely for their 'political inclinations'. Some people have been arrested simply because of their smile.

If anyone wants to read a back issue

Classic Uruguayan torture. The man must sit like that for hours

The generals and admirals are already jockeying among themselves as to who will be that candidate, toying with abolishing the presidency altogether and ruling by junta if the electoral process looks like getting out of control.

This military Frankenstein, remarkably, was given a guarded welcome by much of the world's press when it gently, but firmly, eased itself into power behind the then president, Juan Maria Bordaberry, in February 1973.

The army was in the final stages of its extermination campaign against the

All citizens are suspect in Uruguay. No one talks openly in the streets

of a newspaper, they have to go to the police, declare their intentions, identify the article, and prove their ideological compatibility with the régime. The period covered – from 1880 to 1974 – has been officially labelled the 'political century' to differentiate it from the supposed 'New Age' Uruguay is now embarked upon. Inquiring foreign journalists are immediately locked up as spies.

The generals have also rewritten their own rules. They have postponed their retirements, and reinterpreted the law which says Uruguay can only have fourteen generals at any one time, as meaning fourteen is the minimum. Now they can promote all the ambitious young colonels they choose. Those who have complained have been purged. Last December at a nine-day beano at a beach resort they agreed on a scheme whereby Uruguayans will be allowed to vote for one, and only one, presidential candidate in 1981. The country's two main political parties, the Blancos and Colorados, must agree to field the same man. If they don't, Navy Admiral Hugo Marquez pointed out, it would be seen as a sign that 'they are unfit to exercise power'.

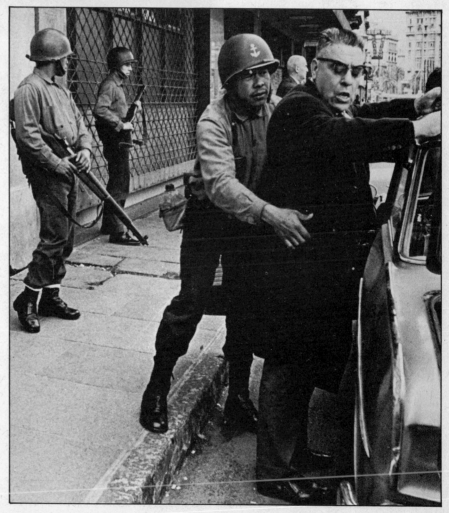

most sophisticated urban guerillas – many of them lawyers, doctors and other professional people – in the world, the Tupamaros. The government had become a bottomless well of stories of graft, corruption and incompetence upon which newspaper readers gorged as they idled in Montevideo's, the capital's, sidewalk cafés, looking for jobs that no longer existed, increasingly jealous of foreign tourists lounging on Uruguay's beautiful beaches.

The military pushed their way into the Cabinet, state airlines, railways and shipping firms, and forced the Minister of the Economy to confess to Parliament that he had coolly and quietly sold off nearly half the country's gold reserves the year before at a ridiculously low price.

Bordaberry eagerly outdid them in fanatical anti-communism. 'This is the hour of the nation, not parties and men,' he declared. But when he suggested setting up his own 'New state' in which 'currents of opinion' would replace political parties, the generals deposed him. First, on 12 June 1976 they replaced him with a seventy-nine-year-old lawyer whom they swore in in five minutes, and three months later with Dr Méndez. At the same time Uruguayan politicians living in exile in Argentina were shot, or disappeared from the Buenos Aires streets, to turn up later in Uruguayan gaols. Assassination squads – members of OCOA (the anti-subversive operations coordinating organization) and SID (defence intelligence service) trained in the United States and Israel – were sent to carry out political murders in Europe. The World Bank, the International Monetary Fund, the Inter-American Development Fund and most American and European banks advanced standby credits, oil facilities and other large loans to guarantee the military's economic programme, written by a disciple of Milton Friedman, the American monetarist who also has advised the Chilean junta.

Uruguay used to be called the 'Switzer-

The 'Guardians of the Nation' – the army defending stability and justice

The government trusts the people, and welcomes them to discuss their daily affairs

land of South America' because it was democratic and prosperous, while all the countries around it were plagued by military coups. Montevideo used to be the intellectual centre of the continent. Now people dare exchange little more than perfunctory greetings in the streets.

Over 400,000 Uruguayans have fled. And over five thousand of the 2.5 million people left are in gaol – giving it the highest per capita rate of political prisoners in the world. They have their heads shaved. And Amnesty International has published photographs of men being tortured – tied naked sitting

on thin rails. The generals merely shrug them off.

The United States, which trained the men in power, formally cut off munitions deliveries. President Geisel of Brazil, which has a fast-growing armaments industry, on the other hand, has publicly reaffirmed he holds the régime in high regard. Self-confessed Nazi sympathizers and known members of 'death squads' have recently been appointed to top government posts and the joint chiefs of staff. Uruguay today is a political morgue.

ZAIRE

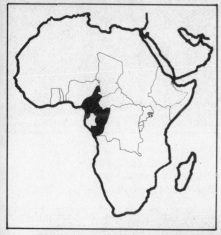

By the end of 1977 President Mobutu, the vain, unsmiling and ambitious ruler of Zaire, had come the full circle. Denouncing the 'criminal and corrupt tendencies in the armed forces' he had assumed direct control of the armed forces without, as he put it, 'intermediaries'. His responsibilities, conferred on himself, covered recruitment, organization, training, discipline and logistics of his ramshackle army.

The announcement carried shades of 1965, when he built up his power base as Chief of Staff to take power of the second largest country on the African continent in a bloodless coup. Since then he has managed to hang on through building up an astonishing personality cult around himself and his party, the *Mouvement Populaire de la Révolution*. To bolster his image the television news is preceded by a shot of him descending, Christ-like, slowly to earth (accompanied by tribal drums). Two years after he made his speech to the UN the TV news bulletins were still peppering the current news items with excerpts from it.

Mobutu's political philosophy is Mobutuism. Mobutuism is 'the thought,

Early days in the Congo. Rebels being beaten to death in 1965

teachings and action of Mobutu'. It has involved a campaign of African authenticity. Names of rivers, streets, etc.,have been changed, as have those of people. Mobutu used to be Joseph-Désiré Mobutu. He is now Sese Seko Kuku Ngbendu Wa Za Banga Mobutu, which means 'the cock who leaves no hen unruffled'. Christmas has been changed to 24 June.

Mobutu's philosophy is a blend of African tribal law and modern communism through his party, the MPR, to which all Congolese belong. He occasionally puts himself to the vote. In December 1977 as the only candidate, he was elected Head of State by the Supreme Court after winning 98.16 per cent of the vote.

This sort of victory has spurred him on to greater efforts towards Mobutuism. Cigarettes in the country are called Zaire, European suits and ties have been banned, along with European music. Mobutuism is a philosophy which works for the good of the country and for Mobutu. His portrait has recently been added to the party badges, and he has ruthlessly and systematically imposed his authority on the twenty-five million people. No opposition is tolerated. Collaborators are dealt with in several ways – a former Prime Minister was publicly hanged, a guerilla leader who returned under an 'amnesty' was shot on arrival.

His autocratic nature has made him fond of staging spectacular show trials of his enemies, which he has said will be 'completely democratic'. He has successively accused Russia, Cuba and the US of trying to topple his inept government, or, as he puts it, of 'attempting to put a spoke in the wheel of the revolution'.

Mobutu has kept comparative calm in his country, the former Congo, which was racked for five years after independence by a series of bloody conflicts when the Belgians departed en masse and left a power vacuum which neither of the rival parties was able to fill. The

The Makuta. Little hedge against the 'crise' and not known as one of the world's most sought-after currencies (*Zaire info. service*)

A non African-authentic Mobutu, complete with European tie and suit drinking to friendship with King Baudoin in Brussels (*Zaire info. service*)

chaos which followed led to the attempted breakaway of the Katanga province and a series of massacres only solved by the intervention of the United Nations and the USSR. The then Secretary General, Dag Hammarskjöld, was killed in a plane crash whilst supervising the operation.

Mobutu has since then had constant trouble with this area, which contains the copper and other minerals which provide seventy per cent of the country's

foreign exchange and sixty per cent of the exports. He has also had trouble with his army.

Apart from backing the wrong side in the Angolan civil war (a mistake hurriedly rectified by making friends with the new ruler), he has found his own 40,000 troops lazy, corrupt and inefficient. In 1975 he denounced their inactivity as 'the scourge of society' and accused the officers – many trained at the US military academy in Virginia and the Royal Military Academy, Sandhurst, England – of failing to work for economic development.

It is needed. The vast size of the country (nearly as big as Western Europe), its strategic importance and huge potential wealth are matched by the extreme ethnic diversity (200 tribes with 700 dialects), an equally large inflation rate and foreign debts of between two and three billion US dollars. The fall in copper prices has not helped.

Mobutu has tried to satisfy the IMF and other international creditors by a series of measures announced last year which brought in the new word of 'asphyxiating' – over-centralization – and pretended to give more authority to the regions. New elections have been held by which MPR candidates have to be voted for at the ballot box rather than just be elected by acclamation at public meetings.

His voraciously acquisitive party officials have been denounced as 'a veritable disgrace' following the scramble for small businesses left vacant by the foreigners he expelled; twenty-eight generals and other senior army officers have been dismissed and his right-hand man, the Foreign Minister, Karl Bond, has been condemned to death for treason. He was given an additional two years for 'insult to the chief of state'. Bond has since been reprieved.

The real reason for the changes has not been so much to please the IMF and the US which backs his government, as to try to purge the humiliation of his army's defeat in 1977, which brought a new nation to add to the Swedes, Italians, Canadians, Belgians, South Africans, Rhodesians, Britons, Lebanese, Greeks and Irish who have variously been sent to Zaire as soldiers and mercenaries to sort the place out. This time it was the Moroccans, paratrooped in by the French to repel an invasion of Katanga which showed up the total incompetence of his army.

In March 1977 a motley collection of 2,000 soldiers, the remnants of the

Read what you can about it. Censored newspapers on sale

Katanga secessionists, marched into the province and proceeded to take control of six key towns. A strange war followed with Mobutu's men, some of them pygmies armed with poisoned arrows, unable or unwilling to find the enemy, whose leader was extensively interviewed on the telephone in Paris.

The US backed off, afraid of embroiling Zambia and Angola, and it was the French who stepped into the breach after Mobutu had been forced to beg for help. They crushed the rebellion, watched by the local people who had refused to give his own forces any support. Some soldiers had been reduced to making a version of porridge in their helmets because nobody would feed them. AZAP, the government news agency, said the operation had 'neutralized certain elements'.

More plots have followed. In March

1978 nineteen out of ninety-one people tried for alleged urban terrorism were sentenced to death. They were said to be in complicity with the Belgians, Libyans and Americans.

Mobutu has been trying to solve his problems with 'autocriticism' to end what has become known in the country as simply 'la crise'. This summarizes the gigantic financial crisis which lies ahead, and which he intends to supervise personally, wearing his authentic African leopard-skin cap, carrying his ivory walking-stick, being referred to in all newspapers and official speeches as 'The President Founder' and 'The Guide', and driving past hundreds of billboards carrying his photograph and the inscription 'Thank you, citizen President'.

The World Dictators' Cup

The rules

1. The nations are split into four qualifying groups. Players select their own order for the group play-offs.

2. The matches are played as follows. One goal is awarded under each of eight headings. Players should assess which dictator, or country, is worst under that category and award the goal to the appropriate side. If both are felt to be equally bad no goal is awarded.

3. The headings are:
   1. Revolting character of dictator
   2. Pomposity and absurdity of dictator
   3. Notoriety of dictator
   4. Cruelty, use of torture and denial of human rights
   5. Curtailment of political activity
   6. Poverty
   7. Quality of life for inhabitants
   8. Hope for future
   Each country with a coup within the last year scores an own goal.

4. When playing each match each country should be re-assessed in comparison with its opponent.

5. In the event of a draw there is a sudden death play-off. The winner is the dictator who came to power by the bloodiest coup.

THE GROUPS

Group 1
Argentina
Indonesia
Iran
Nicaragua
Thailand
Togo
Honduras
Niger

Group 2
Equatorial Guinea
Haiti
Bolivia
Uruguay
Kampuchea (Democratic)
Philippines
Chad
Guatemala

Group 3
Chile
Ethiopia
Pakistan
Paraguay
Bangladesh
Benin
El Salvador
Rwanda

Group 4
Uganda
Brazil
Korea S.
Korea N.
Burundi
Somalia
Zaire
Ghana

Gabon scratched
Central African Empire could not afford the fare

Group
Play-off

Semi-Final

Group 1

```
_____
_____        _____
_____                            _____
_____                                              _____
_____        _____
_____                            _____
_____        _____
```

```
┌────────────────────────┐
│                        │
└────────────────────────┘
            v
┌────────────────────────┐
│                        │
└────────────────────────┘

┌────────────────────────┐
│                        │
└────────────────────────┘
            v
┌────────────────────────┐
│                        │
└────────────────────────┘
```

Group 2

```
_____
_____        _____
_____                            _____
_____                                              _____
_____        _____
_____                            _____
_____        _____
```

FINAL

```
┌────────────────────────┐
│                        │
└────────────────────────┘
            v
┌────────────────────────┐
│                        │
└────────────────────────┘
```

Group 3

```
_____
_____        _____
_____                            _____
_____                                              _____
_____        _____
_____                            _____
_____        _____
```

```
┌────────────────────────┐
│                        │
│                        │
└────────────────────────┘
```

**Where I would most
like NOT to live**

Group 4

```
_____
_____        _____
_____                            _____
_____                                              _____
_____        _____
_____                            _____
_____        _____
```